# 少林功夫

# SHAOLIN KUNGFU

# 《少林功夫》畫冊編輯委員會

## Editorial Committee of *Shaolin Kungfu*

目

## CONTENTS

錄

這是集中了中國武術之精華，帶有神秘的宗教色彩的一種武術流派。從古至今，言武術必及少林。

This is a wushu style which draws on the best elements of the Chinese wushu circles and has a mythical, religious flavor. Since ancient times, people have often related wushu to Shaolin Temple when speaking of martial arts.

# 佛教、禪宗與少林功夫

BUDDHISM, THE CHAN SECT, SHAOLIN KUNGFU

禪功定練省內息止納和足力的少林寺相近之妙

Sitting in meditation, a Shaolin kungfu exercise known only to insiders, is practiced by controlling the breath through concentration.

少林梅花椿功
Fighting on plum-blossom stakes.

武僧朝聖
Fighting monks at prayer.

群僧鬧少室
Shaolin monks practice kungfu on Songshan Mountain

禪武雄風
A photograph of the valiant fighting monks at the monastery.

## 天下功夫出少林

夜幕降臨，一蒙面俠客飛身躍上數丈高牆，隨後悄無聲息地潛入深宅大院……忽然喊聲震天，眾多護院家丁殺奔而出。面對數倍之敵，俠客鎮定自如。但見他微蹲馬步，掌護門心，以不及掩耳之勢迅猛出擊。拳打四路，腳踢八方，一連串"套路"打來眼花繚亂，竟使舞刀弄棍之徒近不得其身……

這是傳統"功夫片"裏的一組鏡頭。作為本世紀六、七十年代與"西部片"同時崛起而風靡於世的一種影片樣式，"功夫片"所創造的仗義行俠的銀幕形象，幾乎與"牛仔明星"一樣整整影響了一代人。然而事實上，那些"飛檐走壁"無所不能的"功夫明星"，在很大程度上只是完成了某些完美無缺的特技動作而已。儘管如此，被西方人稱之為"功夫"的中國武術，卻因此得以廣為世人所知。

正宗的中國功夫也許不象人們在電影裏看到的那般神乎其神，但至少也是令人驚嘆的。在河南鄭州市郊的嵩山腳下，十多個剃着光頭的少林寺和尚，展示了差不多只有在影視片裏借助於特技纔能完成的高超武功 ——頭置地而不倒，槍刺喉而不進，人"上吊"而不死。掌能碎磚，指能碾石，舌能舐火，拳腳更是了得……。作為中國功夫的發源地之一，少林武僧幾乎人人身懷絕技。他們代表的是一種不同於體育表演和影視欣賞範疇的傳統的中國功夫。幾個世紀以來，少林武僧為少林功夫贏得了赫赫聲威，以至於從古至今，一說中國功夫，必言少林

功夫。少林寺也因此而揚名天下。

## 從印度佛教到中國禪宗

與西洋拳擊、朝鮮跆拳道抑或日本空手道不同，少林功夫來源於宗教確切地說來源於佛教，這多少令人有點不可思議。很難想象，本質上屬於暴力和攻擊行為的"功夫"，會和宣揚"大慈大悲"、"積德行善"堅決反對一切"傷生"行為的佛教發生聯繫。在全球成千上萬所佛家寺廟中，少林寺恐怕也是獨一無二以武功而聞名於世的寺廟。

事實上，縱觀世界諸多宗教，除某些原始自然宗教外，大多數神學宗教的內在結構都是排斥強烈的攻擊性行為的，無論是佛教、基督教，還是猶太教，莫不以宣揚禁欲、克制、忍耐、非暴力為其基本的文明素質。少林寺是絕無僅有的一個例外。這一令人費解的現象，解釋起來即使不是十分困難起碼也是很複雜的——

大約在公元前五世紀至公元前四世紀時，也就是孔子、老子等諸多中國思想家"百家爭鳴"的春秋戰國時期，在中國的鄰國（地處南亞的）印度，釋迦牟尼創立了佛教。這是一種包含着強烈的出世、禁欲、苦行和不傷生、非暴力內涵的宗教。其包含了產生痛苦的原因、痛苦的消失、滅苦的方法、現實世界本身的所謂的"四聖諦"教義，實際上是體驗人生之苦的教義。佛教認為世上萬物皆有因緣，概括起來有十一個方面，涉及到諸如對人生的洞察、對理性的反省、對概念的分析等等深奧的哲學。這些在一般人看來十分抽象和複雜的佛教哲學，

幾乎包括了對宇宙萬物的所有解釋。

佛教在印度誕生了四百多年之後，公元前一世紀中葉傳入中國。

由印度傳來的佛教，最初並沒有在中國盛行開來，原因在於印度文化土壤與中國文化土壤的差異所致。

印度文化圈原本與中國文化圈是同存於亞細亞且陸地相連的古代兩大文化圈，但西藏高原和喜馬拉雅山隔斷了它們之間的脈絡，形成了完全異質的兩種文明。不僅氣候、風土等自然條件，而且人種、語言、風俗習慣、社會結構等也顯著的不同，因而最初階段原封不動地從印度照搬過來的小乘佛教，極不適應中國國情，很難為習慣於直覺觀察，感性思維的廣大中國下層勞苦民眾所接受。

這種狀況在達摩創立禪宗之後，發生了變化。

公元527年，印度高僧達摩經海上三年漂泊，來到嵩山少林寺。卓錫於少林寺的菩提達摩，廣收門徒，傳播他所創立的禪宗——一種迎合中國大眾心態或者說已經中國化了的佛教流派，這是一種脫胎於印度佛教，然而其教義和戒律與印度佛教有着很大差異的佛教流派。

禪宗主張靜坐修身、安定養性。倡導"見性成佛"、"頓悟成佛"。禪宗認為人人心中都有佛性，只是由於迷惑而不能成佛。如果信仰佛教、堅持修煉，妄念一旦俱滅，真智自然顯露，於是，內外明徹，悟識本心，遂而成就佛道，獲得真智。在禪宗看來，"見性成佛"全在於"頓悟"、毋須長期修身，也即毋須所謂的"漸悟"過程，也無須遵守一定的戒律，

只要一念覺悟，刹那間即可成佛。

禪宗的這套學說使深奧繁瑣的印度佛教一變而爲適合中國傳統心理的、市俗化的，簡單易懂的中國化佛教，使佛教從嚴格的戒律和修行中解脫了出來。

源於少林寺的禪宗，幾乎寬容殺、淫、搶、盜以外的一切市俗行爲，以至於歷史上出現了孝僧、藝僧、茶僧、酒肉僧等很難爲其他佛教宗派所容忍的市俗僧人。禪宗的這種罕見的宗教寬容環境，給少林功夫的存在和發展提供了一個極爲重要的條件，也爲少林僧人習武敞開了大門。正是在這樣一種獨特的宗教環境之中，少林寺出現了"武僧"。

與一般寺廟裏的和尚不同，少林僧人不講苦行，"壁觀"、"禪坐"即爲修行。達摩以爲面對牆壁，安心靜坐，就能"心爲壁立，不偏不依"，所謂"安靜而止息雜念"。

按照這一教義，達摩身體力行，終日靜坐於五乳峯一天然石洞裏，面壁長達九年，渾然不知鳥兒在其肩膀築窩，身影深投石中。這自然多多少少有後人附會的成份，然而達摩在少林的九年面壁，或多或少爲少林功夫的產生和發展，起到了間接的推動作用。從某種意義上說，少林功夫是禪宗的這種獨特的修行方式的副產品－達摩和他的弟子們爲解除久坐之後的肢體困痲，脾胃不適，不免在"開定"之後，伸臂踢腿，活動筋骨，於是乎便有了少林最初的"武功十八手"。照今天看起來，這更象是某種健身操，然而對於少林僧人來說却並非如此，習武逐漸被看作是修行的一部分，從

而開創了佛教界也許也是宗教界一個不可思議，獨一無二的先例。少林功夫由此開始興盛起來。

## "拒賊""護廟"而成功夫

儘管如此，直至今日有關少林功夫源出何處一直是個引起廣泛爭議的話題。

自達摩開創少林寺祖庭後，禪宗派在中國的傳播十分的迅速，其勢頭遠非諸如成識宗、法相宗、天台宗、華嚴宗、淨土宗這樣一些佛教宗派可以比擬的。唐代以後，禪宗更是成爲中國影響最大的佛教學派，全國各地衆多寺廟中，十有七、八屬於禪宗。

奇怪的是，以武顯名的禪宗寺院，除了少林祖庭以外，再無別處。這固然是由於達摩卓錫少林的緣故，然而更多的原因恐怕還不完全在於此。

事實上，少林功夫的產生是由一係列因素構成的，這些因素大抵是歷史的或然因素碰撞、積澱、聚集的結果。

考中國武術的起源，很容易發現，在久遠的上古時代，民間就形成武功之雛形。不過，那一時期所謂的武功大體上祇是一些捕獵、射禽之類的技巧。然而到公元前後的周、秦、漢，以及此後的三國，兩晉、南北朝時代，武術，也即"功夫"，已作爲社稷的一部分大顯神通。

秦末，陳勝、吳廣農民起義軍以樹枝、棍棒爲武械，大戰王朝軍隊。

漢代，項羽鞍戟率楚軍，稱雄天下；

三國時代，趙子龍單槍破曹營、關雲長用大刀過五關、斬六將，呂布

提戟戰三官；

隋朝年間，小羅成槍挑小梁王……

形成於北魏時代的少林功夫，很大程度上是吸收了民間諸家的功夫之長而形成的。實際上，許多僧人出家前就是武林高手了。少林寺第一代主持跋陀的兩個大弟子慧光，僧稠是少林僧這方面記載的始作俑者。

少林寺的首創者印度天竺高僧跋陀，約早於達摩三十餘年來中國傳經送法。跋陀本人對武術有着濃厚的興趣，至於其是否習武尚無據可查。不過跋陀所收的弟子慧光和稠却都是身懷絕技者。

根據史書記載，慧光和稠皆有異術。慧光年方十二，便能在井欄上反踢鍵子一連五百。稠則擅長輕功，能"橫榻壁行"，輕輕一躍即可到樑。慧光和稠可算是少林寺最早的兩個武僧。

跋陀本人對武術的興趣愛好和他弟子個人的尚武經歷，在少林寺僧的習武歷史上起了關鍵的創始和導向作用，這對以奉祖宗法爲特徵的中國傳統文化環境和戒律甚嚴的佛教環境來說是至關重要的。而此後達摩所創禪宗在少林寺形成的特殊的寬容氣氛，無疑爲這種尚武習俗起了推波助瀾的作用。

不過，跋陀師徒尚武習武畢竟純屬個人的一種愛好，禪宗的寬容也只是提供了產生少林功夫的一塊土壤。促使少林僧人大規模習武，並且得以代代相傳、名聲遠揚的重要原因，還在於少林寺本身的地理位置和特殊的歷史背景。

從大禹傳夏位開始的中國四千年歷史是一部硝煙彌漫，動盪不安的史卷。在長達四千多年的文明記載中，中國社會經歷了無數次的征戰，無數次的割據，無數次的改朝換代。中原腹地由於其地理位置，長期以來便成了中國歷史舞台的中心。地處這一地帶的嵩山少林寺，既有禪宗的寬容環境又有山清水秀、風光如畫的景色，自然而然地成了全國各地的退休將官，不滿朝廷的義傑和逃避官司的壯士最為向往和理想的隱避之所。這其中絕大部分人出家前便是武藝不凡之士。皈依少林寺為僧後，寺眾僧廣，各路武林好手在一個相對穩定而又有節制的宗教環境中，如魚得水，相互切磋，取長補短。博採眾家之長的少林功夫也越發的成熟精煉起來。

促使少林功夫大規模發展的另外一個原因，是出於"護廟、拒賊、防身"的需要。

自南北朝以來，由於歷朝歷代競相舉佛，全國香火鼎盛，寺廟經濟相當的發達，少林寺這樣的大寺院儼然是一座大莊園，不僅有領地，而且還有僱工、僕役。僅開皇年間，隋文帝楊堅就賜田萬畝，供寺僧享用。朝廷的"欽賜"，使得少林僧一反佛教"眾生平等"的基本教義和"托鉢化緣"的宗教行為戒律，成為依靠出租田產和房產為生的寄生階層，這就不可避免地使少林寺卷入到俗家的政治紛爭的狂瀾之中，"拒賊"、"護廟"、"防身"便成了吃齋念佛的少林和尚的一項宗教職責，"武僧"和"僧兵"隨之應運而生。

## "赫赫"僧兵

"武僧"尤其是"僧兵"的出現，表明佛徒習武已為社會所承認，並為統治階層所藉重。自此少林功夫已不僅僅是某些個人的興趣愛好，也不再局限於寺院以內。一個公開的以少林寺為標誌和中心的武術集團和流派開始形成。這是一個集中了中國武術精華、帶有神秘的宗教色彩的武術流派。實戰中，形成了以拳術、棍術和內功為主要內容的武術體係。在這一體係的形成過程中，"僧兵"起了至關重要的作用。

隋末唐初，武德四年（公元621年），秦王李世民與隋將王世充交戰正酣。李世民聞少林僧之悍勇及其宗教號召力，曾專門下詔書要求"法師等亦能深悟機變、早識妙因，克建嘉猷，同歸福地，擒彼兇孽、廓茲淨土"。該書下後，得到少林寺僧響應。於是，"四大皆空"身在"紅塵"外的少林僧人便史無前例地開了佛教徒集體參與戰爭的先河。少林武僧志操、惠陽、曇宗等眾僧兵，搶嶺口一戰，擊潰了王世充軍，助了李世民一臂之力。李世民登基唐朝皇帝後，隆重嘉獎，封曇宗和尚為大將軍，賜少林寺良田四十頃，準於少林寺常備僧兵。少林功夫及其武僧自此揚名於世，少林僧兵逐年興旺。在唐代著名的武僧有善護、志操、惠陽、曇宗、善惠、明高、靈惠、善勝、智守、道廣、智興、豐滿、省仁、覺義、投宏等。宋代著名的武僧有福居、福識、離誠等，元代有緊那羅、福俗、菊庵、息庵、靈庵等。

明代是少林功夫的興旺和發展時期，少林寺僧幾乎全部習武，常住院組成了一支強盛的僧兵隊伍，人數超過二千五百餘名，少林功夫至此形成自己成熟的體係。無論是少林拳，少林器械還是少林內功，都已具有相當水準。明朝廷對少林僧兵十分重視，僅在嘉靖和萬歷年間，就數十次調遣少林僧兵赴邊征寇。最著名的有月空、月行、月靈、已空、悟空、色空、半空、薩空、悟須、周友、周參、洪洪、普使、小山、造化、天地、一舟、大虛、東明、古泉、大用、碧溪、大有、西堂、古峰、普從、宗擎、洪紀、周賀、銘清等。

嘉靖三十二年（1553年）少林僧天真、天池率僧兵四十人於江南"大破倭寇，倭寇走上海"。

同年六月，又有少林僧天員"率諸哨騎為先鋒，月空等排陣於後，與賊戰於白沙灣，大敗倭寇。"此役參戰僧兵超過百人以上。

少林僧兵如此公開的大規模的集體參加戰爭，是少林功夫發展的轉折點。少林功夫開始突破寺院高牆，形成獨特的實戰性強內容廣泛精深的武術體係流傳開去，少林功夫也不再是狹義的寺院功夫了。儘管清代朝廷禁絕僧兵，然而明代創下的少林功夫之盛名，則世代相襲並獨領中國功夫之風騷"夫今之武業，天下莫不讓於少林焉"。

## Shaolin Temple, Origin of All Martial Arts

IT is night. A masked man leaps over the wall and slips noiselessly into the court of a mansion. Suddenly, amidst shouts and curses, guards and servants rush from every door and close in on the intruder. Yet the man betrays no fear; quickly assuming a defensive stance, he strikes out with his fists and kicks his legs in a series of highly sophisticated movements. The cocky guards do not even have a chance....

This is a typical scene from the traditional kungfu film. A prototype of movie contemporaneous with the "Westerns" of the 1960s or 1970s, the kungfu film has created a screen image of a hero like the Western Cowboy who took the audience by storm. Although what the "kungfu star" really accomplishes are no more than some near-perfect stunts, Chinese wushu (martial arts), known as kungfu to Westerners, has thus become popular all over the world.

Real Chinese kungfu may be something quite unlike that projected on the big screen, but it just as amazing. At the foot of Songshan Mountain in suburban Zhengzhou, Henan Province, a dozen monks from Shaolin Temple are demonstrating superb skills normally accomplished by stuntmen only through the aid of modern filming techniques. They stand on their heads, their throats unscathed when pressed against the needle-sharp points of spears. Hanging from the neck, they breathe as usual. They can shatter a pile of bricks with a flash of their palms and mill a stone with their fingers, or lick fire with their tongues. The monks of Shaolin Temple, cradle of Chinese kungfu, are almost all capable of seemingly impossible martial skills, something different from regular sports or the make-believe kungfu represented on TV or in the movies. Over the centuries, they have won fame and prestige for Shaolin, the very name of which has become synonymous with Chinese kungfu.

### From Indian Buddhism to Chinese Chan Sect

Unlike Western boxing, Korean taekwondo, or Japanese jujitsu, Shaolin kungfu has religious origins, rising from Buddhism. This is somewhat contradictory: how can a form of action based on attack and violence be related to Buddhism, which preaches mercy and benevolence and is opposed to all manner of "destruction of life?" Of the world's countless monasteries and temples, Shaolin is probably the only one known for its martial arts.

As a matter of fact, with the exception of certain primitive beliefs, the majority of existing religions are opposed to violent, offensive behavior. Buddhism, Christianity, or Judsism all advocate forbearance, patience and non-violence. With the exception of the Buddhists of Shaolin Temple, Why?

Around the 5th or 4th century B.C. when confucious, Lao Zi and many other Chinese thinkers ex- pounded their teachings during the Spring and Autumn Period, Sakyamuni founded Buddhism in India. Rising as an expresson of opposition to Brahmanism, which was practiced by the Indian upper caste, Buddhism advocated asceticism, non-violence and renunciation of the world. Its "Four Holy Truths" expounded the view that life is pain, analyzed the causes of this pain and provided methods for eliminating it. Buddhists believe that everything has cause and principle. The religion delves into such profound problems as insight into life, introspection on reason, analysis of conception, and provides explanations to a myriad things in the universe.

More than 400 years after its birth in India, Buddhism found its way into China in the 1st century B.C., but did not prosper due to the cultural differences between the two countries.

Although Indian culture coexists with Chinese culture in Asia just as India is connected with China by the continent, their physical relations are severed by the Tibetan Plateau and the Himalayan Mountains. The two countries have different natural conditions and social customs, different races, languages and social structures. Thus the Hinayana form of Buddhism, brought into China wholly intact, did not suit Chinese conditions and was not well received by the Chinese working people.

The situation changed after the

founding of the Chan Sect by Bodhidharma, a holy monk from India. He crossed the ocean and arrived in China in 527, finally settling in Shaolin Temple on Songshan Mountain. There his many disciples listened as he preached a new school of Buddhism — the Chan Sect — which differed substantially from Indian Buddhism and more adapted to the popular Chinese culture.

The Chan Sect advocates self-cultivation through seated meditation. It preaches that everyone has the potential to become a Buddha, but fails to do so only because of obstacles in the mind. If one puts one's faith in Buddhism, banishes all improper thoughts and persists in cultivating oneself, true wisdom can be gained and Buddhahood attained. To a Chan Sect devotee, "instant awakening" is of primary importance.

The Chan Sect thus transformed the abstruse, overelaborate Indian Buddhist tenet into a sinicized form of Buddhism that was adapted to the traditional Chinese psychology. It tolerates almost all forms of worldly behavior except killing, looting, robbing and sex. As a result, Shaolin Temple allowed numerous artist monks, tea or wine imbibing monks and even carnivorous monks not accepted by other Buddhist schools. Such unusual religious tolerance provided an important basis for the existence and development of Shaolin martial arts. Hence the appearance of the "fighting monks" and "cudgelling monks."

Unlike their counterparts in other monasteries, the inhabitants of Shaolin Temple payed little attention to ascetic living. Nor did they study the Buddhist scripture. Their daily routine consisted of "sitting cross-legged in front of the wall" in perfect composure, in order to stifle all distracting thoughts, as preached by Bodhidharma.

It is said that Bodhidharma sat facing the wall in a rock cave for nine years, unaware of birds nesting on his shoulders, his shadow cast deep into the rock face. Perhaps this is exaggerated, but his perseverance provided stimulus to the rise and development of Shaolin martial arts. Long periods of sitting still obviously cause great discomfort and cramped limbs; one needs to limber up to restore circulation. Thus the "18 routines of Shaolin wushu" were invented. By modern physycal standards, these routines are no more than warm-up exercises. But in those days they served as a regular part of the self-cultivation regimen of Shaolin, setting an unprecedented example in the world of Buddhism, or perhaps even in other religions. Shaolin martial arts began to flourish.

## From Temple Protection to Martial Arts

Today, however, the origin of Shaolin kungfu is still a widely debated topic.

After Bodhidharma established his first religious court at Shaolin Temple, the Chan Sect spread rapidly in China, unmatched by the Chengshi, Faxiang, Tiantai, Huayan and Pure Land sects. After the Tang Dynasty, the Chan Sect became far and away the most influential Buddhist school in China, dominating more than 70 percent of Buddhist temples throughout the country. Yet of all the temples professing the Chan Sect, only Shaolin was renowned for its martial arts. Why? There are various reasons, some historical and some coincidental.

As a matter of fact, the first elements of wushu had taken form since time immemorial, through activities such as fishing and hunting. By the Zhou and Qin era, and throughout the Han, the Three Kingdoms, the Western and Eastern Jin and the Southern and Northern Dynasties, wushu began to play an increasingly important role in warfare. At the end of the Qin regime (221-207 B.C.), peasant rebels led by Chen Sheng and Wu Guang fought the Qin army with staffs and tree forks while Xiang Yu, king of Chu, lorded it over every other claimant to the throne with his halberd. During the three Kingdoms Period (220-280) Zhao Yun charged Cao Cao's camp single-handedly and Guan Yu, brandishing his broadsword, forced his way through five cities, hacking down six enemy captains. And during the Sui Dynasty, Luo Cheng slew Prince Liang with an upward tilt of his spear.

To a great extent, Shaolin wushu, which really took shape during the

Northern Wei Dynasty (386-534), drew upon different folk schools of wushu. In fact, before embracing the Buddhist faith, many of Shaolin monks were wushu masters.

Ba Tuo, who founded Shaolin Temple, came to China from India 30 years before Bodhidharma. He had a keen interest in wushu; while it is not known whether he himself ever took part in wushu training, his disciples Hui Guang and Seng Chou were armed with consummate skills.

According to historical records, while still a lad of 12, Hui Guang could kick a shuttlecock 500 times in a row while standing on the rails round a well; and Seng Chou could "walk a wall" and leap up to a rooftop with one bound. They were the first Shaolin monks to practice martial arts. But what contributes to Shaolin monks' mass participation in wushu training is the temple's geographical location and special historical circumstances.

During the 4,000 years in the recorded Chinese history, from Yu the Great of the Xia Dynasty (2100-1600 B.C.) up to the last Qing Dynasty, Chinese society endured innumerable wars, factionalist rulers and changes of regimes. Over the centuries, because of its geographical position, the Central Plain had always been the center of the Chinese historical stage; and Shaolin Temple, with its tolerant atmosphere and picturesque surrounding, became an ideal haven for retired generals, malcotents and refugees from the law from all over the country. Before embracing the faith, however, most of these people were recognized wushu experts. As they came together, they had the opportunity to trade special skills, and gradually Shaolin wushu became considerably more mature and refined.

Another factor leading to the advance of Shaolin wushu was the need to "protect the temple against marauding bandits."

After the Southern and Northern Dynasties (420-581), monasterial economies expanded drastically due to the court's growing interest in Buddhism. Shaolin Temple not only had its halls and extensive grounds, but also its employees and attendants. Emperor Wen Di of the Sui Dynasty (581-618), for example, granted Shaolin 1,648 acres of land for the sustenance of its members. Such imperial graciousness knocked the bottom out of the basic Buddhist tenet that "all forms of life are equal," and turned the monks into something of a parasitic class dependent on the leasing of land and housing for a living. Inevitably, Shaolin monks found themselves involved in the whirlpool of political struggle. In order to protect their temple against banditry, monk-soldiers were born.

### "Illustrious" Monk Soldiers

The appearance of the monk-soldiers indicates that the concept of devotees participating in wushu training was accepted by the society and supported by the ruling class. Shaolin wushu was no longer a matter of personal taste and interest, nor was it kept hidden within the walls of the monastery. A wushu clique and style was formed, with Shaolin Temple as its nucleus, which drew on the best elements among the Chinese martial arts circles. It specialized in boxing, cudgelling and internal exercise, with Shaolin monks taking a leading role.

In 621, between the late Sui and the early Tang, a fierce struggle unfolded between the Qin prince Li Shimin and the Sui general Wang Shicong. Hearing of the Shaolin monks' prowess, Prince Li issued an edict calling upon the monks to "help apprehend the prime culprit and pacify the land." The monks responded, the first time ever that Buddhist disciples had collectively taken part in battle. In the campaign of Qianglingkou, Shaolin monk-soldiers routed Wang Shicong's army. Prince Li was enthroned as the Tang emperor, he awarded the Shaolin monks handsomely, conferring the title of Great General on monk Tan Zong and granting Shaolin Temple 40 hectares of land. Moreover, the temple was permitted to retain a standing army of monk-soldiers. From that time on, the Shaolin troops became widely known, and their ranks grew from year to year. Among the famous fighting monks in the Tang Dynasty were Shan Hu, Zhi Cao, Hui Yang, Tan Zong, Shan Hui, Ming Gao, Ling Hui, Shen Sheng, Zhi Shou, Dao Guang, Zhi Xing, Feng Man, Jue Ren, Jue Yi and Tou Hong. Renowned Song Dynasty (960-

1279) fighting monks included Fu Ju, Fu Shi and Li Cheng, and those of the Yuan Dynasty (1271-1368) were Jin Na Luo, Fu Su, Ju An and Ling An.

The Ming Dynasty (1638-1644) saw a blossoming of Shaolin martial arts as never before. Almost all the residents of Shaolin took up wushu and a powerful detachment of over 2,500 monk-soldiers was organized. Shaolin wushu had come into its own, whether in boxing, weapons or internal exercise. The Ming government treasured the monk-soldiers, sending them on expeditions to border areas several dozen times between the reigns of emperors Jia Jing and Wan Li. The most well-known fighters of this era included Yue Kong, Yue Xing, Yue Ling, Si Kong, Wu Kong, Se Kong, Ban Kong, Sa Kong, Wu Xu, Zhou You, Zhou Can, Hong Hong, Pu Shi, Xiao Shan, Zao Hua, Tian Chi, Yi Zhou, Da Xu, Dong Ming, Gu Quan, Da Yong, Bi Xi, Da You, etc.

In 1553, forty Shaolin monks led by Tian Zhen and Tian Chi "inflicted a crushing defeat on Japanese pirates." In June of the same year, "pioneered by patrols led by Tian Yuan and supported by rearguards led by Yue Kong, Shaolin monks fought and defeated Japanese pirates at Baishawan." More than 100 monk-soldiers took part in the battle.

The mass participation of Shaolin monks in military campaigns marked a turning point in the development of Shaolin wushu, which evolved into a comprehensive system strongly combative in nature. Despite the Qing government's eventual suppression, Shaolin kungfu has remained a leader among Chinese wushu circles.

作爲少林功夫的主
體和核心，少林拳簡練
實用，而其套路則蘊含
着某種莫測高深的東方
哲理。

As the main body and
nucleus of Shaolin kungfu,
Shaolin boxing is simple and
practical, with routines that
embody a profound Oriental
philosophy.

"悟性"
就在脚下……

ENLIGHTENMENT IS
ACQUIRED THROUGH
SELF-CULTIVATION

# "守之如處女，犯之如猛虎"

這是少林拳在實戰運用中的一大特色，作為組成少林功夫的主體和核心，少林拳產生的歷史可以上溯至一千多年前的北魏時代，也就是達摩創禪宗的時代。寺僧們為解除"禪定""靜坐"之後的不適而習練的"羅漢十八手"，便是少林拳的雛形。然而一直到明末清初少林拳才真正形成自己的特色和套路。這比少林功夫中的器械功夫晚了很多。少林拳術從發展到成熟，經歷了一個漫長的歷史進程。

少林拳初創時僅有"羅漢拳"一種。依據少林拳譜上的說法，羅漢拳是少林諸多拳路的核心和鼻祖。由於少林寺深居山林，為防猛獸的襲擊，眾僧根據禽獸和人們生產勞作中的各種動作，又發展了"心意拳"。在當初，寺僧習拳主要目的在於防身和健身，尚未構成完整的少林拳路。

自少林武僧助唐有功，朝廷恩準大規模習武後，少林拳開始了較快的發展。飽嘗功夫甜頭的少林寺倡導眾僧習武，大力發展拳術。寺主鼓勵武僧出山巡遊四方，訪師求藝，廣泛吸取全國各地武術高手之精華，取長補短，遂而演變成為少林拳。宋代時，方丈福居禪師就曾邀請全國十八家武林高手，會集少林寺交流獻藝，演練三年，滙成《少林拳譜》廣授僧徒。使少林拳路一下子增至二百八十餘套。宋代開國皇帝趙匡胤據傳說就因得過少林真傳，而使其長拳打得爐火純青。

金、元時期，覺遠和尚出山西行，在蘭州、洛陽訪到武術高手白玉峰、李叟，同歸少林寺切磋武功。在少林十八手的基礎上又新創了少林拳七十餘手，而後又發展到一百七十三手。與此同時，覺遠和尚根據三國時期的名醫華佗的"五禽戲"，創立了少林五拳—龍拳、豹拳、蛇拳、虎拳、鶴拳，並且發展了搏擊技藝，使得少林拳術逐漸形成了自己的特色。

到明、清兩代時，不少仁人志士感於國事日非，投少林寺而去，以圖來日報國，遂將眾多民間拳路帶入寺院，而清代的朝廷習武禁令，又使武僧離寺四散，流落各地，少林功夫卻因禍得福，得以在俗家廣為普及，流亡僧人晚年重返山門，便把寺外所學別門之長也帶入了寺院，少林拳愈臻精混，到清末時，少林拳達數百種之多，以後屢遭摧殘，拳術大都失傳。流傳至今的尚有小洪拳、大洪拳、通臂拳、炮拳、羅漢拳、猿拳、七星拳、心意拳、柔拳、梅花拳、太祖長拳、黑虎拳、伏虎拳、蛾虎拳、螳螂拳、醉拳、連三錘、陰風拳、十八滾、十八翻、羅漢十八手、飛花拳、提手炮、蓮花拳、大炮錘、關鐵門、昭陽拳、連環拳、蓮花拳、長護心意門拳、反臂張掌、追風掌、夜叉鐵沙掌、少林八法拳、八陣拳、八極拳、五虎拳、猛虎拳、豹子拳、狗拳、蛇拳、太祖教掌、心意長拳、羅漢十八拳、五子拳、看家拳、金剛拳、金石拳、破連拳、地熬拳、五風拳、灰狼拳、風火拳、飛沙掌、流星錘、格斗拳、六合拳、五虎群羊等一百多套。

少林正宗拳術包括外功拳和內功拳。其風格剛勁勇猛，凌厲疾速，節奏緊湊而鮮明。少林拳素以"剛"和"硬"見長，人們常常把少林拳稱之為"硬拳"。然而這種"剛"和"硬"僅僅是就少林拳的外在感覺而言。實際上少林拳恰恰是極重"柔勝"和"智取"的。少林拳講究的是以剛為主，剛中有柔，剛柔相濟。其力量的運用靈活而富有彈性，內靜而外猛，所謂"守之如處女，犯之如猛虎"。

少林拳打起來不受場地限制，幾步之內便能發揮威力，因而有"拳打臥牛之地"一說。少林拳的特點極為鮮明，從拳譜"身法八要"上講，起、落、進、退、反、側、收、縱都始終在一條綫上進行，因而其攻擊性和防守性都很強。從純粹功夫的角度講是一種簡練、實用的拳法。

少林拳的基本支柱是手、眼、身、法、步。其手法曲而不曲，直而不直，滾出滾入、運用自如，其眼法注目為鶴，審度敵勢，其身法起橫落順，轉動靈活，著重掌握重心，不失平衡。其步法進步低，退步高，抬腿踢腳，輕如掠鴻，重如落鼎，不強求放大弓、馬步形，求其自然，少林拳的一招一式，一拳一腿，非攻即守，攻中有守，守中有攻，虛虛實實，變幻無窮。值得一提的是，中國武林中長期以來有"南拳北腿"之說，屬北方派的少林功夫，在拳路上卻毫不遜於南派功夫，而其腿腳的運用，則首屈一指，這使少林拳術運用起來更爲自如，也更具有實戰意義。

## "首爲悟性，次爲健體，末爲防身"

也許是由於與宗教有緣的關係，集百家之長的少林功夫儘管吸收了眾多民間俗家的武術內容，然而與民間武術又不儘相同，少林功夫不僅有其本身的武術體係，而且有着寓意深刻的文化體係和思想體係。

在少林武僧看來，少林功夫"首爲悟性，次爲健體，末爲防身"。心誠則靈，心誠，"悟性"也就在你腳下了，習武之人有了"悟性"才能眞正理解少林功夫的意義。

佛家所說的"悟性"，也就是人們在內心深處對一種事物本質上的領會能力。佛家認爲，把握佛理需要有悟性，有了悟性，才能眞正認識世界、感受宇宙萬物之靈性，少林功夫中的"悟性"，就是要求習武之人把握功夫之"神"，理解其中的眞髓。也就是通過習武，在理性上領悟某些人生

哲理、修煉自身的德行、情操，最終達到身心的平衡。一如"靜坐"、"面壁"所要達到的境界。在少林武僧看來，只知其外在招式而不知其內在寓意、爲武而武的功夫是膚淺的，最多只是一種"花架子"功夫。只有"神形兼備"的功夫，才是眞正的功夫。少林拳中的"套路"便是這種思想的直接反映。

與一般人們印象中的拳擊、擊劍、摔跤等等技擊運動不同，少林拳有着眾多的"套路"。簡單地說，這是一些有着內在聯繫，互相連貫着的動作，就象是某種程序。然而這些套路決不是簡簡單單的幾個武打動作而已，這也正是少林功夫與一些"花拳繡腿"功夫的區別所在。少林拳術的每一個套路，幾乎都有着一定的含意，都是某種思想的反映，而套路中的每一個動作又是這種思想的組成部分。儘管這些思想往往不是所有人都能領會的，而且顯得虛無飄渺，但卻常常蘊含着哲理。實際上這多少也反映了中國人對宗教思想的一種理解，一種人對天和地、身和心、理和性的民族化的理解。這種理解與諸如"天地之作"、"陰陽之合"、"欲擒故縱"、"福兮禍所伏，禍兮福所依"等等將人類活動與宇宙自然相對應和聯係看問題的反映中國傳統世界觀的格言俗語是一脈相承的。

例如屬於少林秘不外傳的保守

套路之一的著名的少林"金剛拳"，其套路不僅複雜，而且極爲講究。金剛拳打起來"變如雲、行如龍、猛如虎"。其"套路"五十二招式，幾乎招招富於深刻寓意—猛虎出洞、金鵬展翅、野馬分鬃、懷中抱月、倒踢北斗、魁星抱斗、餓虎登山、雀地龍走、元帥傳令、梨花舞袖、紫燕鑽雲、白猿孝母、野馬行空、老君封門、將軍勒馬、金龍旋雲、閉門推月、老虎望洞、大鵬展翅、野馬彈蹄、仙人望洞、麒麟亮勢、過關斬將、羅漢鐵臂、金鵬斜展、金豹扣爪、大鵬斜飛、白猿獻書、二郎擔山、青龍盤爪、羅漢鑽井、天鵝下蛋、黃忠搶關、綳手擺蓮、鴻門射雁、迷糊攪手、羅漢還禮、羅漢合十……世界萬物之生存法則，被精練地濃縮到了"套路"之中，從而使拳路被賦予了某種靈性的東西而得到了昇華。

## "In Defence, like a Virgin; in Attack, like a Tiger"

As the nucleus of Shaolin wushu, Shaolin boxing dates back more than 1,000 years to the Northern Wei, when Bodhidharma founded the Chan Sect. In those times, the monks were practising the "18 routines of *Luohan* Boxing" to relieve the fatigue and cramped sensations of long hours in meditatiom, but it was not until the late Ming or early Qing Dynasty that Shaolin boxing won fame among wushu circles for its special characteristics and routines. This was much later than the development of Shaolin kungfu with weapons.

In its initial stage Shaolin boxing was represented solely by *Luohan* Boxing, the nucleus and origin of all the various routines of Shaolin boxing. To defend themselves against the attack of wild animals, Shaolin monks created the *Xinyi* (Heart-and-Mind) Boxing, mimicking the actions of animals and human labor. But this rudimentary practice was still far from being an integral system of Shaolin boxing routines.

Shaolin boxing began to develop rapidly following the Tang court's patronage and permission for large scale wushu training. The benefits brought by wushu prompted temple authorities to encourage monks to take part in serious wushu training and to tour the country, seeking out masters for advanced training and exchanging knowledge with wushu fans. During the Song Dynasty, Fu Ju, abbot of Shaolin Temple, invited experts from 18 wushu schools to Shaolin for an exchange of skills. They

remained for three years and ultimately edited the *Shaolin Boxing Manual* which described 280 routines. It is said that Zhao Kuangyin, founding emperor of Song, was able to thoroughly master the routines of Long Boxing because of what he had learned at Shaolin.

During the Jin and Yuan dynasties, monk Jue Yuan descended the mountain and traveled west. In Lanzhou and Luoyang he met experts Bai Yufeng and Li Sou, and returned with them to Shaolin for further exchange of wushu skills. Subsequently, more than 70 routines of Shaolin boxing were created on the basis of the 18 routines of *Luohan* Boxing, which developed further into 173. Meanwhile, mimicking the "Five-Animal Play" devised by the famous physician Hua Tuo of the Three Kingdoms Period, Jue Yuan created the Dragon, Leopard, Snake, Tiger and Crane boxings and developed the art of attack.

During the Ming and Qing dynasties, a group of highly idealistic people aware of the deteriorating political situation joined Shaolin Temple, with a view to dedicating themselyves to the service of the country at a decisive historical juncture. They brought with them countless folk wushu routines. At the same time, the Qing government's ban on the practice of wushu caused many Shaolin monks to leave the temple and roam the country, thus bringing Shaolin wushu to a popular level. Returning to the temple in later years,

these monks brought back what they had learned from other schools. By the end of the Qing Dynasty there were several hundred types of Shaolin boxing in current use. Though some have been lost since, more than 100 sets of sparring methods have survived. They include *Xiaohong, Dahong, Tongbi* (Long Arm), *Pao* (Cannon), *Luohan, Yuan* (Monkey), *Qixing* (Seven-Star), *Xinyi* (Heart-and-Mind), *Rou* (Soft), *Meihua* (Plum Blossom) and many other boxings.

Genuine Shaolin boxing includes both internal and external exercises. They are rigorous, hard-hitting, quick and fierce, going by the name of "hard boxing." But of course this is only its superficial aspect; in fact, Shaolin boxing accentuates soft tactics, combining both "hard" and "soft." "In defence, like a virgin; in attack, like a tiger."

The practice of Shaolin boxing is not subject to the size of the court; it can give play to its power within a few paces. "Room enough for an ox to lie down will suffice." All movements—up and down, forward and backward, withdrawing and advancing and sidestepping—proceed along a straight line. It is therefore both highly defensive and offensive, and from a pure wushu standpoint, both simple and practical.

The basic elements of Shaolin boxing involve the hand, eye, body and foot. Hand movement should be neither entirely crooked, nor entirely straight, but must be flexible. The eyes should be fixed on the enemy, observing his intentions. The body should be pliant and well balanced. In footwork, maintain a low posture in advance and high posture in retreat. When kicking out, the foot should be as light as a bird or as heavy as a falling tripod. Every movement contains either attack or defence, or both. Feinting or real, it changes all the time and is highly unpredictable.

Among Chinese wushu circles the current view has been that the "strong point of the southern school lies in the use of the fist, while that of the northern school is footwork." But Shaolin is an exception. Though belonging to the northern school, Shaolin boxing is by no means inferior to the southern school, while in footwork it is definitely number one.

## The Power of Understanding, Keeping fit, Self-Defence

Although Shaolin kungfu is a potpourri of folk wushu, it also includes a profound cultural and ideological content.

To a Shaolin fighting monk, the power of understanding is more important than keeping fit and self-defence. And if one is sincere, one has the power of understanding at one's fingertips. Only then will one be able to realize the significance of Shaolin kungfu.

In Buddhism, the power of understanding means the ability to grasp the essence of things. A Buddhist believes that to grasp Buddhist theory and truly know the world, one needs to have the power of understanding. In the case of wushu training, one has to grasp its spirit and understand its essence. In other words, one needs to understand the philosophy of life through wushu practice, finally attaining a balance of mind and body similar to the state of mind reached in sitting still. To a Shaolin monk, knowing a routine without understanding its inner meaning—wushu practiced for its own sake—is only skin-deep knowledge. It is at best a showy performance. Kungfu is genuine only when it combines both form and spirit.

Unlike other kinds of boxing, swordplay, or wrestling, Shaolin boxing consists of numerous routines with continuous, organically connected movements. In contrast to the "flowery boxing and embroidered footwork" style, each routuine contains a profound meaning. It is a reflection of specific thoughts—man's understanding of heaven and earth, body and mind, reason and feeling.

The noted *Jinggang* (Dvarapala) Boxing, for example, contains sophisticated routines known only to devotees. Its action is "quick as lightning, fierce as a tiger and changing like the clouds." Each of its 52 routines is pregnant with meaning—a long dragon leaving its cave, golden roc spreading its wings, embracing the moon, kicking the Big Dipper, a hungry tiger climbing up the mountain, the marshal dispatching his orders....

The law of existence for the world's myriad things has been crystalized and incorporated in these ancient routines.

少林三十三代武僧釋永壽演練鷹爪拳"雄鷹捕食"

"A hawk springing on its prey," a pose, from Hawk's Claw boxing, as demonstrated by Shi Yongshou, a 33rd-generation fighting monk of Shaolin Temple.

①

②

## 少林"像形拳"

①鶴拳
②龍拳
③豹拳
④狗拳
⑤蛇拳
⑥鴨拳

Imitative Shaolin boxing:

(1). Crane boxing.
(2). Dragon boxing.
(3). Leopard boxing.
(4). Dog boxing.
(5). Snake boxing.
(6). Duck boxing.

③

④

⑤

⑥

①

①飛脚断棍
②釋行直，少林三十二代武僧。
③少林僧釋行鷹演練少林醉拳

(1) Breaking the cudgel with a flying kick.
(2) Shi Xingzhi, a 32nd-generation fighting monk of Shaolin.
(3) Shi Xingying, a resident of Shaolin, practices drunkard's boxing.

③

①

②

①"青龍探掌"
②少林鐵頭功
③"怪蟒翻身"
④少林擒拿

(1). "The black dragon stretching its claws."
(2). The iron-head, a routine of Shaolin kungfu.
(3). *Guaimangfanshen*, or "a python overturns its body."
(4). Wrestling and catching.

③

④

①

①一英戰雙雄
②大洪拳
③少林三十四代武僧釋延孜擅長搏擊，曾多次
　獲得全國散打冠軍。

(1). One takes on two.
(2). *Dahong* boxing.
(3). Shi Yanzi, one of the Shaolin's 34th-
　　generation fighting monks, is versed
　　in the art of attack and has won the
　　national free-sparring title on many
　　occasions.

塔利飛戰
Fistfighting in the Forest of Pagodas

以棍揚名的少林器械功夫，伴隨着歷史的年輪，已是明槍暗箭，十八般兵器樣樣健全了。

Over time, weapons exercise, which owes its rise to fame to the cudgelling art, has developed into an exercise with various types of weapons.

"八仙過海，
各顯其能"
"EIGHT IMMORTALS
CROSSING THE SEA,
EACH SHOWING
HIS OR HER PROWESS"

# 十三棍僧救唐皇

公元621年,也就是隋末唐初交替的年代,自封爲鄭王的隋亡朝大將王世充,在河南嵩山一帶與秦王李世民率領的唐王朝征討軍展開了激烈的交戰。經過數日大戰,新興的唐王朝軍隊陣前失利,李世民被俘。唐軍遂求助少林寺。長久以來對王世充強佔少林寺大片土地深惡痛絕的少林寺僧,即刻響應徵召。以曇宗、志超、惠陽爲首的十三個武僧,攜棍出山,只一場伏擊,十三棍僧便擊潰鄭軍,生擒敵帥王世充侄兒王仁則,並且救出秦王李世民。感恩戴德的李世民登基後便大封大賞少林寺僧。從此以後,少林棍開始揚名於世,成爲少林最爲知名的代表性器械。"十三棍僧救唐王"也成了少林歷史上流傳最爲廣泛的一段插曲。此後,以棍揚名的少林武僧頻頻的參與了俗家戰爭。明嘉靖癸丑年(公元1553年)由月空和尚率領的一支四十人組成的僧兵隊伍,再次出山,開赴江南沿海抗擊來自東瀛的倭寇。少林僧兵人手一根七尺長,三十多斤重的鐵棍,所向披靡,一時令倭寇聞棍喪膽。

然而,少林棍術最初的揚名起於抗擊農民起義軍騷擾的過程之中。這多少有點諷刺意味。與中國歷代農民起義軍所做的一樣,隋代末年名震一時的"紅巾軍"倡導"殺富濟貧"。富甲一方的少林寺自然也在劫難逃。一時大兵壓境,危急時刻,竈下僧緊那羅操起一燒火棍,以勇不可擋之勢,大戰來軍,進而成功的退敵於山下。緊那羅也被稱爲少林棍僧的祖師爺。

少林棍在實戰中的運用開了少林器械運用的先河。直到今天,少林兵器功夫中依舊以棍術爲最精深和知名。不過嚴格地說,少林棍原本並不屬於兵器類。從理論上講,也正是因爲棍棒不屬兵器,才得以與少林拳術一樣發展到今天這樣的程度,並成爲少林功夫的主導部份。佛家以慈悲爲懷,戒鬥戒殺。刀、槍、劍一類兵器離不開銅鐵鋒刃,唯有棍既非金鐵、也無鋒刃,不屬戒律之內,因而最適宜佛門弟子攜帶,只是歷史的因素常常使事物在發展過程中偏離原來的軌道。事實上,少林棍不僅廣泛地參與了戰爭,最後甚至被引進了明代朝廷的軍隊,成爲使用廣泛的兵器。

少林棍術簡練實用,可謂一棍在手,萬夫近不得其身。少林拳打一條綫,而棍則打一大片。少林棍打起來呼呼生風,棍到敵倒,恰好似秋風掃落葉。

少林棍術講究步法、腿法、跳躍、翻轉平衡。雲、掃、劈、挎、戳、削、點、摔是其基本棍法。少林棍的種類很多,盡管歷史上失傳了許多,傳至今天的仍有齊眉棍、風火棍、齊天大聖棍、六合聖手棍、小梅花棍、雲陽棍、排棍、小夜叉棍、少林愈家棍、單盤龍棍、雙盤龍棍、猿猴棍、大夜叉棍、穿梭棍、上沙排棍、中沙排棍、下沙排棍、齊天棍、羅王棍、燒火棍、滾星棍、細女穿綫棍、飛龍棍、五虎羣羊棍等近三十種。

# 少林武藝十八般

自十三棍僧救唐王之後,少林僧兵逐年增加。唐、宋王朝還常派將官到少林寺切磋武藝。這些將官在向少林武僧學藝的同時,也把自己的特長武技傳授給了寺僧們,如程咬金的月牙斧、羅成的梅花槍、高懷得的黑虎銅錘、楊家將的二十一名槍等都先後傳入少林寺。經過千百年反復實踐、發展,諸多種類的兵器,使得少林器械功夫"異軍突起",獨成風格。

少林器械功夫分爲棍、槍、刀、劍、戟幾大類,即所謂的少林"十八般兵器"。少林十八般兵器最初分爲"九長""九短",宋代以後,發展到了二十多種,現在常用的有斧、棍、槍、戟、矛、大刀、鐺、劍、勾、拐、鞭、三節棍、流星、九節鞭、飛鏢、匕首、錘等,也許是由於歷史上有過濃厚的"軍事色彩"的緣故,少林器械功夫實戰性很強。在當初,少林僧兵出征,往往順手便抄起一件"家伙",無論是棍、劍或者是刀,甚至於板凳,只要一件器械在手,武僧們常常便能以一當十,勇不可擋。

少林兵器中,除了棍以外,當屬

槍、刀、劍三種最爲著名，並和棍一起被稱爲少林“四大名器”。

所謂“槍”，當然並不是現代意義上的火器，只不過是在棍的頭上加了一個鋒利的戟。少林槍以“扎”爲主，攔拿爲輔。槍尖直出直入、力達於槍尖，謂之“槍扎一條綫”。槍法有崩、穿、點、挑、撥、掃、戳及舞花等。少林槍術曾有這樣一個口訣：“出槍如放箭，收槍如撥箭，挑槍如雲翻，壓槍似捺虎，跳步如登山，眼要隨槍轉，牢記槍中訣，制敵有何難”。在尚未有火器運用的情況下，槍與棍等兵器在歷史上被稱之爲“長兵器”。長兵器使用起來能拒敵於數步之外。因而在武術界有“保命槍”一說。相對於槍、棍這類長兵器而言，刀則屬於短兵器。少林刀術從其套路及其歷史記載來看，是僅次於棍棒的器械。其套路不下百種，實戰運用中似如猛虎，八面威風，因而有“捨命刀”一說。少林刀術分爲“單刀”和“雙刀”。刀法有纏頭裹腦、劈、刺、掛、撩、砍、戳、攔、挑等。

與中世紀西方宮廷裏的劍客不同，少林劍術演練起來缺乏那種貴族的騎士風度，然而其劍法相信絲毫不在這些騎士之下。少林劍術也許是少林諸兵器中最能體現東方人風格的一種兵器：莊重中顯出靈秀、優雅中透出英武，自始至終以“行雲流水”般的韻味來展示高超的劍術。“劍行如飛燕、劍落如停風、劍收如花絮、劍刺如鋼釘”。大約是少林劍術的這些獨特之處，歷史上，少林劍更多的是被用於日常習練，而非戰爭。武僧們常常以習劍爲磨練韌性和品性的方式。

不過少林武僧日常卻並不總是持槍携棍的。他們更多的是携帶各種形狀奇特的短兵器，諸如三節棍、繩鏈、飛鏢、達摩杖、鐵笛、鐵扇等等。這些短兵器是少林特有的稀有兵器，其中許多屬於暗兵器。格鬥時往往能起到常用兵器所不能起到的作用，令人防不勝防。

暗器的使用，使少林器械功夫如虎添翼。正所謂“明器能防，暗器難躲”。

## Thirteen Shaolin Monks Rescuing the Tang Emperor

As the Sui Dynasty gave way to the Tang Dynasty in 621, Wang Shicong, a Sui general under the assumed title Prince Zheng, was engaged in a fierce battle with the Tang army led by Li Shimin in Henan's Songshan Mountain area. After several days' fighting the Tang army was defeated and Li Shimin taken captive, whereupon the Tang army sent a message to Shaolin Temple begging for help. The temple authorities who had always resented the seizure of their land by Wang Shicong, responded immediately with 13 monks. Headed by Tan Zong, Zhi Chao and Hui Yang, the cudgel-bearing monk-soldiers descended the mountain. and they fulfilled their mission — they ambushed and routed the Zheng army, capturing Wang Shicong's nephew and rescuing Li Shimin. After Li ascended the throne, he rewarded the Shaolin monks handsomely. the cudgel has since become Shaolin's most celebrated weapon and the "rescue of the Tang emperor by Shaolin monks" a widely circulated episode from the history of the monastery. Shaolin monks have since taken part in many campaigns.

In 1553, during the Ming Dynasty, a company of 40 monk-soldiers led by Yue Kong determinedly marched down the mountain, on their way to the southeastern coast to fight the Japanese pirates. Each armed with a 7-foot, 15-kilogram solid iron staff, the monks swept through the enemy ranks, striking terror into the hearts of the Japanese marauders.

Ironically, the Shaolin cudgel owes its reputation to its use as a defensive weapon against peaseant rebels. Like many peasant rebels throughout Chinese history, the Red Turbans of the late Sui Dynasty advocated "plundering from the rich to give to the poor." Shaolin by far the wealthiest monastery in Henan, was naturally targeted as a victim. But when the peasant army appeared before the temple gate, Jin Na Luo — a monk who tended the stove — grabbed his fire stoker and laid it about him with such fearlessness and vigor that the Red Turbans scattered in utter confusion. Jin Na Luo became known as the first of the Shaolin cudgelling monks.

The cudgel was the first weapon ever actually used by the wushu practitioners of Shaolin Temple. Even today the art of handling the cudgel is still the most profound and best known of any other weapon practiced at Shaolin. Strictly speaking, the cudgel is not a weapon, and thus was allowed to develop as an integral part of Shaolin martial arts, along with boxing. Buddhism, being opposed to killing and fighting, frowns on the use of sharp weapons such as the sword and spear. But the edgeless cudgel is tolerated. As a means of self-defence, it is ideal for a Buddhist disciple. Eventually it was widely employed in battle, and even included in the Ming's armory.

Shaolin cudgel techniques are simple and practical, and can be applied to one's great advantage in self-defence. Bare-handed, one can deal with one or two people, but armed with a cudgel one can hold off a whole group of attackers.

The art of Shaolin cudgelling emphasizes footwork — leaping, somersaulting and balancing. although today many of the methods have been lost, nearly 30 have been preserved, including *Qimei* (Eyebrow), *Fenghuo* (Wind-and-Fire), *Qitiandasheng* (the Monkey King), *Xiaomeihua* (Little Plum Blossom) and *Feilong* (Flying Dragon), to name just a few.

## The Eighteen Types of Shaolin Martial Arts

The generous bounty bestowed upon Shaolin Temple after its rescue of the Tang emperor allowed the ranks of the monk-soldiers to swell rapidly from year to year. Tang generals were often sent to exchange routines with Shaolin monks. Generals Cheng Yaojin, Luo Cheng, Gao Huaide and the Yang family members, for instance, taught the monks their characteristic fighting skills with the crescent axe, the plum blossom spear and the black tiger hammer. After repeated practice and research, Shaolin monks were able to develop different types of weapons and form their own unique styles.

There were originally 18 types of weapons used by Shaolin monks, divided equally between the long and short, which eventually increased to over 20 after the Song Dynasty. Today they include the common axe, cudgel, spear, halberd, sword and broadsword, square, lash, 3-section staff, shooting star, dart, dagger and hammer. Colored by its long "military" tradition, Shaolin techniques are strongly combative in nature. When a Shaolin monk went to battle, he could pick up anyting at hand—a cudgel, a sword, a broadsword, or even a bench—and effectively hold off a dozen men.

Among the 18 types of Shaolin weapons, the most famous and representative are the cudgel, spear, sword and broadsword, known together as the four major weapons of Shaolin.

The Shaolin spear is employed primarily to stab, but can also be used to parry. When feinting with an enemy, the monk is able to send his strength straight through to the spear tip. The old formula for Shaolin spearing techniques is as follows: "Launching a spear is like releasing an arrow, while withdrawing it is like drawing a sword. An upward tilt is like clouds rolling, while a downward thrust is like holding a tiger by the scruff of its neck. Leaping with a spear is like climbing a mountain, with the eye following the spear's movement. If you commit these rules to memory, you will have no difficulty overcoming the enemy."

Before firearms were in use, the spear and cudgel were known as "long weapons." As the spear can hold off an enemy at a dozen paces, it

was known as the "life-saving spear." The sword and broadsword, on the other hand, belonged to the "short weapons" category. The Shaolin broadsword, as evidenced from its routines and historical records, ranked just after the cudgel, commanding more than 100 routines and wielding enormous power in actual combat. The broadsword can be used singly or doubly.

Unlike the knights of Western courts of the Middle Ages, Shaolin swordsmen lacked the aristocrat's graceful poise. Technically, however, the Shaolin sword player is by no means inferior to his European counterpart; the Shaolin sword is probably the weapon which best expresses the pure style of the Orient. But in actual combat, the sword continuously moves like a writhing dragon from one routine to another, "quick as a flying swallow and hard as a nail." In daily training, it is primarily used for the tempering of the mind and the development of tenacity, rather than for actual fighting.

In general, however, Shaolin monks did not carry only swords or cudgels in their daily pursuits; more often they were armed with all sorts of odd-looking short weapons hidden on the body, such as the 3-section staff, Bodhidharma staff, dart, iron flute and iron fan, many of these being unique to Shaolin. These played extremely specific roles and were difficult to ward off.

The use of hidden weapons gave the Shaolin monks additional power over their enemies.

月牙斧"凌空飛腳"，少林三十四代釋延明。

Kicking while standing upside down by holding onto the axe shaft, a movement of the art of the crescent axe, is seen in the picture demonstrated by Shaolin's 34th-generation fighting monk Shi Yanming.

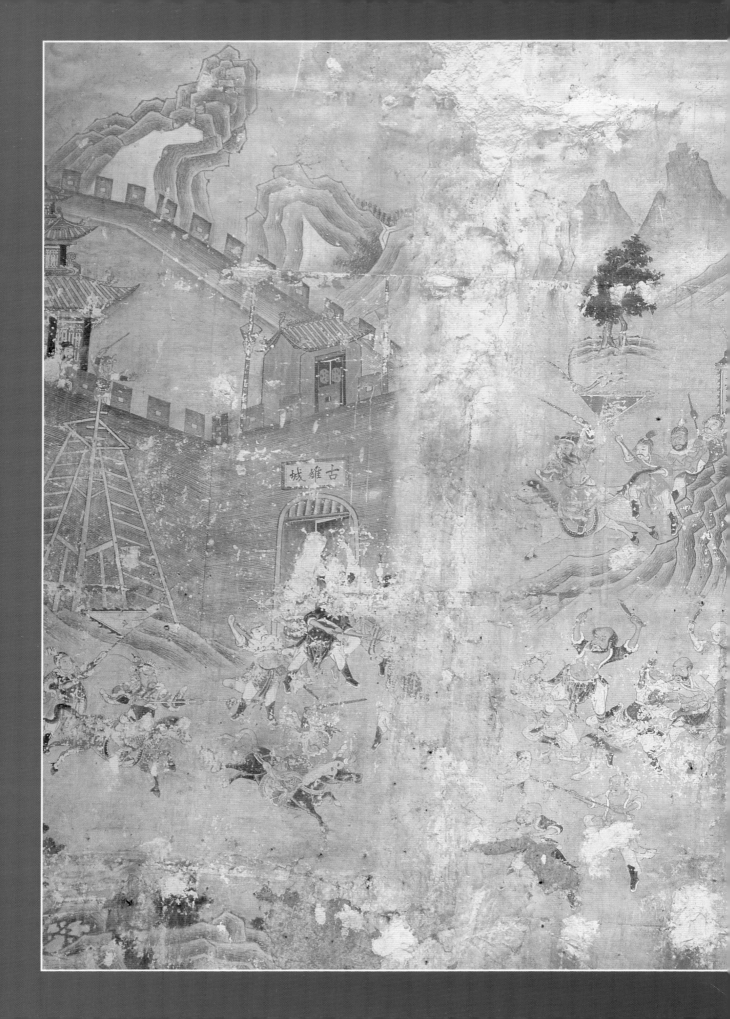

壁畫"十三棍僧救秦王"。

The mural *Thirteen Cudgelling Monks Rescue the Qin Prince*

少林群棍
Cudgelling monks at Shaolin Temple.

① ② ③ ④

①少林三十一代僧德陽，通曉佛法擅輕功和拳械。

②達摩杖

③"飛檐走壁"

④春秋大刀

⑤釋德成凌空飛刀

⑥虎頭雙鈎

(1). De Yang, a 31st-generation monk of Shaolin, is well versed in Buddhist doctrines as well as in light exercise and weapons exercise.
(2). Bodhidharma staff.
(3). Fighting up and down the cliffs as if they were on flat ground.
(4). A monk wields a spring and autumn broadsword.
(5). Shi Decheng adopts a stance with his broadsword.
(6). A pair of tiger-head hooks.

①

①少林三十三代僧尼（女僧）釋永梅精通拳械
②大刀破槍
③釋德道，少林方便鏟。
④月牙鏟"回頭望月"

(1). Shi Yongmei, a 33rd-generation nun, is an expert in barehand exercise and weapons exercise.
(2). One versus one.
(3). Shi Dedao and his *fangbian* shovel.
(4). Thrusting back with a crescent shovel.

① ②

①少林單刀
②三尖兩韌刀
③少林暗器"飛鏢"
④對少林武僧來說樣樣是兵器
⑤三人大戰

(1). A monk waves a single broadsword.
(2). The tri-point double-edged sword exercise.
(3). Darting.
(4). To the fighting monks of Shaolin, anything can be used as a weapon.
(5). The three are locked in fierce struggle.

①群僧小憩
②少林鐵扇功
③月牙斧

(1). A break from training.
(2). The art of the iron fan.
(3). He is armed with a crescent axe.

兩節棍
Two-section cudgel play

"練武不練功，到老一場空"。武和功的結合，令少林武僧幾乎人人身懷絕技。

"Your efforts will be futile if you fail to practice martial arts and breath control simultaneously." The combination of the two helps almost all the monks of Shaolin grasp sophisticated wushu skills.

"軟如綿、輕如燕、硬如鋼"

"SOFT AS COTTON, LIGHT AS A SWALLOW, HARD AS STEEL"

## "少林七十二藝"

自唐代以後，以棍術和拳術爲特色的少林功夫聲譽日隆、影響日盛，這種勢頭到清代雍正、道光年間開始消沉下去。來自於異族的滿清統治者唯恐漢族臣民習武而生事非、殃及朝廷，遂降旨：刀槍拳棍一律不準習練，違者殺無赦。在如此高壓政策下，民間似乎再無人敢習武了。少林武僧自然拳不練了，棍不耍了，然而每入夜晚，萬籟俱寂，少林古刹便顯現另一種景象。但見千佛殿內一字排開玉米斗、鐵沙斗、石頭、磚塊、沙袋……在教頭僧的指揮下，武僧們或運氣丹田、或拳擊鐵沙……偷偷地操練着武藝，所不同的只是改拳棍爲氣功罷了。衆僧在習練氣功的同時，暗暗地把氣功中導引引氣的某些功法與技擊結合了起來，進而形成了獨具特色的少林內功。少林內功不僅吸取了中國道教內丹修煉的一些理論和方法，而且引進了中國醫家的經絡學說。在此基礎上，少林功夫體係中最爲精華的一部份——少林絕技誕生。

少林絕技被認爲是少林武僧的看家功夫，秘不外傳，大體分爲內功、輕功、硬功、童子功、椿功、點穴功、擒拿功、打擂功等等。統稱爲"少林七十二藝"，計有三十六種外功、三十六種內功。

"少林絕技七十二種"可謂各有千秋，各具功力。中國古人認爲，人之所以能生存，其理全在氣與血調和、陰陽平衡。若氣血失調，則骨不壯、筋不柔。少林氣功實際上便貫徹了這樣一種思想。精通少林氣功之僧，不但能以氣制人、槍刀不能損，並且可強身健體，延年益壽。

少林氣功通常可分爲軟硬兩種、內外二功。所謂內氣功，是通過內氣的吐納和調息來達到以氣制人或者健身養性之效。少林功夫中的"一指禪"即屬此類。指到之處，人必死、無藥可醫。少林外氣功也稱"硬功"，主要是通過運氣將內氣聚集於身體的某一部位，使這部位發出異常的功力。這種功力往往超出了人們的想象力。就一般人而言，如果不是親眼目睹，大約很難相信這樣的事實：鐵棍擊肚而紋絲不動、百斤大石吊於睾丸而面不改色、舌舔爐鐵而不皺眉頭………而所有這些令人難以置信的硬功夫，只不過是少林看家功夫中的一部份。

據記載，早在"少林七十二藝"形成完整的體係之前，少林就已出現了少數身懷絕技之僧。擅長輕功的大弟子稠，可算是少林歷史上最早的氣功大師了。宋代端宗年間，首座僧洪溫大和尚，耄耋之年尚能頭頂百斤之物，雙膝架人。元代的惠榘和尚和明代的行正和尚，皆能隔牆制熄炬、丈外制人………

也許是少林功夫特有的傳統的訓誡緣故，少林絕技沿襲到今天，儘管失傳了一部份，但大部份得以保留了下來。少林武僧於拳械之外幾乎人人都有一、二手"絕活"。對於少林武僧來說，軟硬絕技功夫與拳術、器械功夫猶如耳之於目，不可有須臾分離。正是在這種思想指導下，才會有"打拳不練功，到老一場空"的古老訓誡。

## "梅花椿"、"童子功"

這是少林絕技中最具代表性的功夫，其技巧最爲高深，非三五年甚至十數年不能練就。

少林梅花椿功屬於輕身功夫的一種，這種功夫要求有敏捷的身手、靈活的步法和絕佳的眼神。木椿面積很小，一般高出地面近兩米，相隔一定距離，分爲"五星椿"、"八卦椿"、"九宮椿"等數種。在此椿上格鬥稍一疏忽，便有掉下椿頭的危險，而少林僧卻常常能如履平地。

由"易筋經"和"八段錦"演化而來的"童子功"則屬於少林外氣功的一種，是少林諸功中最令人驚嘆的功夫。這種功法難度極大，練就後不僅身體各部位"軟如綿、輕如燕、硬如鋼"，而且可以鶴髮童顏、返老還童。少林功夫中一些著名的功法諸如"二指禪"、"倒栽碑"、"抱佛腳"、"朝天蹬"等皆屬童子功的範圍之列。

## The Seventy-Two Hand-Combat Arts of Shaolin

The Shaolin martial arts began to decline after the middle of the reign of Qing emperor Yong Zheng. Concerned that wushu training would cause unrest and violence amongst the Han people and affect the stability of the court, the Manchu rulers outlawed all types of weapons training, on pain of death. The high-handed policy effectively deterred the practice of most martial arts; the monks were forced to put away their swords and cudgels. Still, when night descended and all was still, neatly marshalled vats and jars of corn and iron sand, piles of stones and bricks, and sandbags lined the Thousand-Buddha Hall. With the guidance of monk-instructors, Shaolin monks would practice breath control by holding their breath in the abdominal area, or hitting the iron sand with their bare fists.

As early as the Northern Wei (286-534), Shaolin monks had incorporated Taoist theory and practice concerning the preparation of elixirs. They often drew upon the *jingluo* theory of traditional Chinese medicine, which conceives the human body as covered by a network of passages, known as the main and collateral channels, through which the vital energy circulates. It was by combining such breathing techniques with boxing that the 72 hand-combat arts, the best of Shaolin kungfu, were born.

These consummate skills are regarded as strictly secret, never to be divulged to outsiders. They consist of 36 internal exercises and 36 external exercises including light exercise, hard exercise, child's exercise, walking and fighting on top of stakes set into tle ground, freezing an enemy by jabbing his acu-points, over-powering an enemy barehanded. Each of these sophisticated techniques has its own strong point.

Shaolin breath control can be divided into the soft and hard, or internal and external exercises. Internal breath control exercise is practiced either as a means to subdue an enemy or as a way to keep fit and cultivate moral conduct by regulating the internal *qi*. One example is *yizhichan* (headstand on one finger). Anyone who is jabbed by that finger is sure to die. Shaolin external breath control exercise stresses directing the internal *qi*, through concentration, to a certain part of the body, thus endowing it with extraordinary strength, so powerful and incredible that it is beyond people's imagination: standing absolutely still when the abdomen is hit by an iron staff, remaining calm without even batting an eyelid with a 50-kg. stone block hanging from the testes, maintaining perfect composure while licking a burning hot iron fresh from the furnace....

According to historical records, a number of monks with superb wushu skills had appeared at the temple prior to the formation of the complete system of 72 hand-combat arts. Seng Chou, who was skilled at light exercise, was the earliest master of breath control at Shaolin. Though advanced in age, Hong Wen, abbot of Shaolin Temple during the reign of the Song Dynasty emperor Duan Zong (1276-1278), was able to carry a load of 50 kg. on his head. Both monk Hui Ju of the Yuan Dynasty and monk Xing Zheng of the Ming could subdue an enemy from several meters away.

Thanks to the strict traditions enforced at the monastery, most of the consummate skills of Shaolin kungfu are alive today. Every fighting monk mastered one or two unique routines of breath control, in addition to their command of boxing and weapons exercise. Their theory held that boxing and weapons training can not be conducted without practicing breath control. The ancient exhortations say, "your efforts will be for naught if you fail to combine boxing with breath control."

## Plum-Blossom Stake, Child's Exercise

A light exercise, the plum-blossom stake requires dexterous body movement, quick footwork and sharp eyes. The stakes stand some two meters above the ground and each is set at a specific distance from the others. According to strict geometry, the stakes can be placed in Five-Star, Eight-Diagram and Nine Palace formations. And Shaolin devotees are able to fight on top of the stakes as if they were moving on solid ground.

The child's exercise, the most amazing and difficult of all Shaolin kungfu, is a kind of breath control. Anyone who has mastered the skills will feel rejuvenated, with limbs as soft as cotton, light as a swallow and hard as steel.

少林火功 "舌舔紅鐵鏟"

Licking a burning hot iron shovel: one of the most difficult skills of Shaolin kungfu.

①

①武僧釋延鵬少林童子功之一 "倒栽碑"
②武僧釋延武少林童子鐵襠功（又名千斤墜）；
　此功是少林散打必修之功，練此功須從童子
　時開始，久練方能抵禦各種打擊。
　　　　上圖拖動五百餘斤重的石滾，下圖為睪
　丸系繩吊起五十餘斤重的大石塊。
③少林童子功之一 "二指禪"

(1). *Daozaibei*, (headstand without support), a routine of the child's exercise performed by the fighting monk Shi Yanpeng.
(2). Fighting monk Shi Yanwu is doing *tiedanggong* (iron crotch exercise). Also known as *qianjinzhui* (one-thousand-*jin* plummet), it is compulsory in the training for free-sparring. One must start this practice in childhood; only after years of effort can one stand attack. Top right on the facing page shows Shi pulling a stone roller weighing more than 250 kg. The picture at bottom right shows him heft a 25-odd-kg. stone block attached to his testes with rope.
(3). *Erzhichan* (headstand on two fingers), one of the many extremely difficult routines of the child's exercise.

②
③

鐵布衫

He is able to withstand heavy blows as if he were wearing a *tiebushan* (iron jacket).

①

②

③

## 少林武僧全身皆功：

①手指劈磚
②頭頂斷磚
③腿勁碎磚
④肘部砸磚
⑤手臂開磚

The fighting monks at the monastery are armed with kungfu from head to foot:

(1). Cutting through bricks with his fingers.
(2). Smashing bricks piled on his head.
(3). Smashing bricks on his leg.
(4). Shattering bricks by elbow.
(5). Breaking with one hand bricks held in the other hand.

① ②

①少林絕技"鐵頭功"（俗稱"上吊功"），此功須有專人指導方可演練。

②鐵牙功

(1) *Shangdiaogong,* or hanging from a tree with a rope round the neck, is considered basic training in Shaolin wushu. It should be trained under the direction of an instructor.

(2) *Tieyagong,* or lifting a bicycle with the teeth.

①

②

①少林氣功,圖中兩手相擊處可見明顯氣場,這
　是少林秘不外傳內氣功法。
②少林小氣功——拔碗,碗扣腹部武僧運氣之
　後數人之力無法拔起。
③少林童子功"抱佛脚"

(1). Breath control exercise of Shaolin. A
     qi (vital energy) field can be seen
     where the two hands clash — a secret
     ability never exposed to outsiders.
(2). Sucking the bowl is a routine of
     Shaolin's breath control exercise. The
     combined strength of several men
     can not pull away the bowl from the
     practitioner's abdomen when he
     directs his strength to that part of his
     body.
(3). Baofojiao (forward bend), a routine
     of the child's exercise.

③

頭頂砸甕
Breaking a vat with his head.

①

①少林小沙彌釋行野年僅八歲練有一定功夫，
　師傅在其頭頂砸核桃，毫無懼色。
②少林武僧釋德虔擅長鐵肚功
③曾獲得國際少林武術散打冠軍的武僧釋行乾
　苦練爪功。

(1). Shi Xingye, 8, has already mastered
some kungfu. He remains calm as his
master crushes walnuts on his head.
(2). She Deqian, a fighting monk, is adept
in *tiedugong,* or iron abdomen
routine. He holds his ground even as
a tourist strikes with all his might at
Shi's belly.
(3). Hard at training his fingers. Shi
Xingqian once won the free-sparring
title at an international Shaolin
wushu festival.

②

③

①少林童子功"葉下藏花"
②少林輕功基本功訓練

(1). *Yexiacanghua* (squatting on one leg), a routine of the child's exercise.
(2). Basic training in the light exercise of Shaolin kungfu.

②

小沙彌在練梅花站樁功
A child novice on the plum-blossom stakes.

"冬練三九、夏練三伏"，唯苦恒爲徑，方得一生眞功。

Year round training with no rest, even in the dog days of summer and the coldest days of winter. Hard training and perseverance are the way to learn real kungfu.

"臥如弓、走如風、坐如鐘、站如松"

"SLEEP WITH THE BODY BENT LIKE A BOW, WALK SWIFTLY LIKE THE WIND, SIT CROSS-LEGGED LIKE A BELL, STAND FIRMLY LIKE A PINE"

## 禪影伴燈苦恒爲徑

"日練千斤脚、霎時飛毛腿，繩星疾跳澗，游綾飛懸崖，若知其中妙，鐵瓦纏十年。"這是清代少林著名大師貞俊留給當今後生僧一本手抄本拳譜中記載的話。貞俊大師六歲入寺爲僧。八歲始隨師傳學功，歷經數個春秋，最終練得一身高超輕功，縱步可上房，飛崖能越澗。拳譜中的這段話便是大師習武的感受。從某種意義上說，這也正是少林功夫的真諦所在。

事實上，無論是少林拳、少林器械還是少林絕技功夫，樣樣都是靠異乎尋常的、有時候甚至是令人不可置信的苦練換來的。例如達摩開創的"禪坐"，常常令僧人盤腿打坐一連數小時甚至數天。直到今天，這種坐禪方式依舊是少林內功的必修之課。武僧按禪法坐定後，腦與心、眼與耳必須很快進入空無狀態，任憑雷聲震天、刀追頭腹，不僅聲色不動，而且禪位形體不改。這就要求練功之人晨四時即起，夜半更深再起作禪，以便思純心專、氣易領發。如此反復演練堅持不懈、方能進入少林功夫之門。

與內功相比，少林外功的訓練近乎於一種自我折磨。無論是掌功、拳功、腿功、指功還是頭功，差不多每一次都練到皮開肉綻才罷了。初練伊始，這些部位常常血肉模糊。正是靠這種差不多殘忍的苦練，少林武僧獲得了一身錚錚鐵骨。著名的"指鑽牆"硬功，初練時每天指插米斗五十至一

百次，二、三月後，轉爲指插沙粒；疼痛異常而不能停練，只到再生一層皮時開始插鐵砂，每日三百至五百次，即便皮破血流也不得停手，久而久之指端便生出一層較厚的痂繭。經過多次傷而癒、癒而傷、指痂增厚、勁充猛、氣疾達、血更壯氣、硬漸如鋼、鋒如鐵叉，此時便可鑽壁入洞，功遂練就。這是一種意志的磨練。少林衆多令人驚嘆的硬功夫皆是這般練就的。

少林功夫的這種習練之"苦"，非一般人可以承受。少林有這樣一種說法：練三年肉掌可以分磚；練十年單指可鑽牆成洞，練三十年兩掌如銅似鐵；練四十年可折斷樑柱。而少林童子功則更是終身相投，尤不得近女色，一朝不慎，前功儘棄。

對功夫的這種全身心的投入，令少林武僧格守着與衆不同的"威儀"——臥如弓、走如風、坐如鐘、站如松。這種威儀爲少林功夫增添了某種獨特的魅力。

## "習武先習德、
## 笑顏迎人欺"

對於少林武僧來說，苦練功夫的全部概念遠不止於習練武藝本身，它還包括了培養習武之人的德性和操行。這甚至於是比武藝更重要的一個方面，

只有擁有了高尚德行，加以苦心研練、持之以恒，才能真正成爲武林高手。聞名本世紀三十年代的武林高手少林第二十九代大和尚貞緒大師，就曾寫過一篇習武戒約："武德有良師、苦恒出高手。習武先挨打、笑顏迎人欺。寧可受人打，決不先打人。持技做歹事、辜負先師心。"戒約反映了中國傳統的道德思想，這與佛家思想有某種相通之處：尚德不尚力。力雖足以傷人，而人未必心悅誠服，唯德者，力雖遜於人，而人必帖然。因而，凡屬少林賢徒弟子，習武必先習德，摻禪精佛、恒習書文、默誦戒約以保持少林宗風。無技無德者，非少林之徒。因而少林武僧和寺外皈依門徒，雖武藝超羣，但歷史上除了幾次特殊的戰爭之外，很少顯露於世。

## Sitting in Meditation in the Lamplight, Hard Training and Perseverance Are the Way to Learn

"If you persist on practicing with pieces of iron tied to your legs every day, you will eventually become fleet-footed, capable of jumping over mountain streams or leaping onto cliffs like a shooting star. What is the secret? The answer lies in 10 years' perseverance." These are the lines in a hand-written manual composed by Zhen Jun, an eminent Shaolin wushu master of the Qing Dynasty. Zhen became a monk at Shaolin Temple at the age of six and began practicing wushu at eight. After years of training he eventually acquired superb skills in light exercise, able to leap onto rooftops and jump over mountain cliffs with no difficulty. The above-mentioned lines express his understanding of wushu, after a lifetime of training. In a sense, the lines indicate the true essence of Shaolin martial arts.

As a matter of fact, Shaolin boxing, weapons exercise and the high-level skills of Shaolin kungfu only can be mastered through extremely, almost unimaginably hard training. For instance, the monks were often seen sit cross-legged in meditation, initiated by the Indian monk Bodhidharma, for hours or even days at a stretch. Even today this is compulsory in the internal exercise training at Shaolin Temple. In meditation a monk sits still, with his mind, heart, eyes and ears ignoring his surroundings. He holds his ground despite roaring thunder and swords pressed to his throat. The monks are required to get up at 4 o'clock in the morning for meditation and resume sitting again at midnight, for at these quiet hours they can practice with undivided attention. They will eventually learn the rudiments of Shaolin wushu, but only after constant practice and unremitting effort.

Compared with internal exercise, external exercise is almost masochistic. No matter what they employ — palm, fist, leg, finger or head — almost all the practitioners, especially the beginners, find themselves cut, bruised and bleeding at the end of a day's training. It is only through such hard, in a sense, cruel training that they can become strong both in will and body. Take zhizuanqiang (boring the wall with a finger). The monks begin by thrusting their fingers into a jar filled with rice 50 to 100 times a day. Two to three months later, they shift to using sand, not quitting even though it is extremely painful to the fingers. When the skin peals off and new skin appears, they practice in iron sand 300 to 500 times daily. In this way, a hard layer of callus eventually forms on the finger tips. As the calluses thicken, the thrusting power of the fingers increases, enough to bore holes in a wall. This is a will-tempering exercise; in fact, all the skills of the Shaolin hard exercise are learned this way. The monks practice day and night, rain or shine, in short, the year round.

It is difficult for ordinary people to endure such long years of hardship. A saying at the temple goes, "A palm can smash bricks after three years' training, a single finger can make a hole in a wall in 10 years' time, a fist will become as hard as an iron hammer after 30 years' practice, and a hand can break a wooden column in 40 years' time." The Shaolin child's exercise requires one's lifelong devotion and forbids any sexual activity, otherwise all previous effort will be wasted.

The Shaolin monks throw themselves wholeheartedly into training. They follow four guiding principles: sleeping with the body bent like a bow, walking swiftly like the wind, sitting cross-legged like a bell and standing firmly like a pine; these add a unique bit of charm to Shaolin wushu.

## Cultivate Moral Integrity Before Practicing Wushu, Take Bullying with a Smile

To the Shaolin monks, hard training is simply not enough. More important is the cultivation of moral integrity. Only by pursuing noble morals and a spirit of hard and persistent training can they become wusu experts. Zhen Xu, the 29th abbot of the monastery, was an eminent figure among the wushu circles of the 1930s. On wushu training, he wrote, "One will become a master wushu artist if he trains hard and persistently and fosters moral integrity under a good instructor. As a wushu practitioner he should take beating and bullying with a smile and should rather be beaten than strike the first blow. If he does evil things with the skills he has learned, he will be unworthy of the instructor's original intention." This reflects a certain traditional Chinese moral outlook, which is similar to the Buddhist thought — advocating morality instead of strength, for strength will never convince others. All the able and virtuous residents of Shaolin Temple, without exception, first learned to footer noble ideals before taking up wushu training. Though they were extremely skilful in martial arts, the Shaolin fighting monks and their disciples in society seldom revealed their skills in public except for the few military campaigns in which they participated.

演練頭頂功
Hardening their heads.

少林鐵砂掌功基礎功之一"拍手功"
Beating water in a vat is part of the basic
training for the iron sand palm exercise.

頭頂倒立是"倒栽碑"功的基本功，久練人
可凌空倒立。

Headstanding, a basic training method in
*daozaibei*. Years' perseverance in training
will enable the trainees to stand on their
heads without any support.

① "冬練三九、夏練三伏"，少林功夫就靠這
　種毅力練出來的。
② 少林內功 "心意拳" （少林著名看家拳）
③ 倒掛金鐘

(1). They persist in training year round,
     even during the dog days of summer
     and the coldest days of winter.
(2). Heart-and-Mind boxing, an internal
     exercise of Shaolin.
(3). *Daoguajinzhong*, or hanging upside
     down.

②

③

晨起即練，腿綁鐵瓦苦練輕功。

After getting up early in the morning, they tie pieces of iron round their legs for the light exercise.

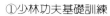

①少林功夫基礎訓練
②鐵掌就是這樣練出來的
③少林僧接待客人也是一種練功，手中鐵壺重
　達百斤
④雪地練馬步功
⑤吃飯也在練功
⑥嚴師出高徒

(1). Basic training in Shaolin kungfu.
(2). This is the way to turn his hands into iron.
(3). Offering tea to the guests is also part of the training: the kettle weighs as much as 50 kg.
(4). Practicing horse-riding stance on snowy ground.
(5). They do not suspend training even while eating.
(6). A severe instructor will train his disciple to be a good wushu practitioner.

鍋沿上練輕功
Light exercise training on the edge of a cauldron.

當少林功夫再一次爲世人矚目時，其概念已不僅僅是原有的含義了。功夫成了中國文化的一個方面而得到了前所未有的普及。

When Shaolin kungfu once again became the focus of world attention, it surpassed its orginal function and meaning. As a representative of Chinese culture, it has witnessed unprecedented popularity.

# "佛法無邊、香火縈繞"

INFINITE POWER OF BUDDHIST DOCTRINES, NUMEROUS WORSHIPPERS AT THE TEMPLE

以少林武僧爲代表的少林功夫發展到今天，實際上已遠不僅僅限於寺院了。

在少林寺的山門外，一個接一個的武術學校、學院誕生了，來自全國各地的成千上萬名迷戀於少林功夫的小學生、中學生，一批又一批地湧進了這些武術院校；一座佔地四千四百七十二平方米，以招收"洋"弟子爲主的"少林武術館"，在八十年代中期建成，並與少林寺成比肩而立之勢。這種情形甚至於出現在遙遠的海外異邦。在日本，宗道臣所創"少林寺拳法聯盟"擁有少林"拳士"達百萬之衆；在新加坡，"少衆山國術體育會"影響遍及南洋、會員日衆；在大洋彼岸的美國，"華林寺武術社"僧衆武顯，聲振全美；在阿爾卑斯山脚下，瑞士諾瓦士少林功夫團頻頻地向人們展示其少林拳脚功夫……

少林功夫的這種潮水般的發展規模，很大程度得益於六、七十年代"功夫片"所帶來的影響。以香港已故著名功夫影星李小龍爲代表的功夫片，向東西方世界展示了中國古老的武術技藝的魅力，儘管"功夫片"很大程度上是藝術加工的產物，不過世人卻因此而對功夫產生了濃厚的興趣，這種興趣隨着八十年代初期另一位李姓功夫明星的崛起而掀起了新的一輪高潮。一九八二年，中國大陸與香港合拍的大型功夫片《少林寺》在海內外的上映，令李連傑這一名字和少林功夫一起蜚聲於全世界，鄭州嵩山少林寺成了中國一個新的旅遊熱點，每年湧入山谷習武、觀光、訪問的人流多達一百五十萬人次。少林功夫也越發的普及開去。僧徒和皈依弟子頻頻地受聘任師，海內外各路人馬紛紛而來"歸宗朝聖"。於此同時，以少林功夫爲主的武術比賽、散打擂台賽和大型的少林功夫國際研討會也接連召開。一九九一年秋季舉辦的鄭州國際少林武術節是歷史上最爲盛大隆重的。來自海內外十數個國家和地區的衆多功夫好手滙聚鄭州，進行拳術，器械及散打等諸多項目的比賽，並相互切磋武藝，作爲宏揚少林及中國功夫的一個重要方面，一年一度的鄭州國際少林武術節，將爲中華武術的普及作出獨特的貢獻。

Shaolin kungfu, represented by the temple's fighting monks, has developed to such an extent that it has spread far beyond the temple walls.

Outside today's Shaolin Temple stand one after another school and institute, erected to meet the demand of wushu fans coming from primary and high schools across the country. The Shaolin Wushu Guild, built in the mid-1980s especially for foreigners, sprawls beside the temple, covering an area of 4,472 squre meters. A popular interest in wushu also appears abroad. The Japanese League of Shaolin Temple Boxing, sponsored by So Doshin, boasts 1 million boxing practitioners. The Shaozhong Mountain Martial Arts Association in Singapore has an increasing number of members and its influence extends over the whole of Southeast Asia. The fame of the U.S. Wahlum Temple Wushu Society has spread far and wide in the country. And a Swiss Shaolin kungfu federation founded by Victor Nowas often gives wushu demonstrations to the public....

Shaolin kungfu owes its rapid popularization, to a great extent, to the kungfu movies of the 1960s and 1970s. Li Xiaoling, the late Hong Kong kungfu movie star, showed the world the excitement of time-honored Chinese martial arts. Although the stunts portrayed on the screen are the result of artistic treatment, they helped to arouse great audience interest in kungfu. This interest evolved into a craze when another kungfu star appeared on China's mainland in the early 1980s. In 1982, *Shaolin Temple*, a full-length kungfu film, was co-produced by the mainland and Hong Kong. When it was shown in China and abroad, Li Lianjie, the star, and Shaolin Temple gained world-wide renown, making the temple a tourist spot overnight. More than 1.5 million people throng every year to learn wushu or just to observe. Shaolin monks and their Buddhist disciples outside the temple were engaged as wushu instructors. Meanwhile, wushu competitions and international seminars on Shaolin kungsu were held one after another. The grandest to date was the Zhengzhou International Shaolin Wushu Festival, held in the fall of 1991.

少林三十代高僧素喜打得一手罗汉拳
Su Xi, an eminent monk belonging to the
30th generation, is an able boxer.

少林高僧素雲是少林寺三十代武功的正宗傳人，精通各種少林功夫，現任少林寺武僧敎頭。嵩山少林寺武術館總敎練。

Su Yun, a noted monk at Shaolin Temple and a 30th-generation inheritor of Shaolin kungfu, excels in various wushu routines. He is now an instructor of the fighting monks at the temple and head coach of the Songshan Shaolin Temple Wushu Guild.

少林居士行行精通少林氣功和醫術。

The lay Buddhist Xing Xing is versed in
Shaolin breath control and medical skills.

嵩山少林寺武術館國際教學部部長焦洪波是
精通少林拳械的全能武術名師。

Jiao Hongpo is a well-known expert both
in the barehand and weapons exercises.
He works as director of the International
Teaching Department, the Songshan
Shaolin Temple Wushu Guild.

少林皈依弟子德虔（右）大師，不僅通曉各種功法，而且深諳少林醫道並著有大量關於少林功夫的書籍。

Master De Qian (right) is proficient not only in various wushu routines but also in the art of healing. He has written many books on Shaolin kungfu.

①

③

①少林武術名師梁以荃在演練少林單拐
②美國華林寺少林訪問團，在寺門外表演功夫。
③民間少林拳師張廣俊、崔西奇在研討少林功
　夫。

(1). Liang Yiquan, an expert of Shaolin wushu, practices with a staff.
(2). A member of the United States Wahlum Temple Wushu Delegation gives a kungfu demonstration outside the gate of Shaolin Temple.
(3). Zhang Guangjun and Cui Xiqi, masters of Shaolin boxing, exchange Shaolin kungfu pointers.

②

少林寺名譽方丈德禪大師接見日本少林寺拳法聯盟會長宗由貴，該聯盟現有少林拳士百萬之眾。

Shaolin Temple's honorary abbot De Chan poses for a picture taken with Yoshitak So, president of the Japanese League of Shaolin Temple Boxing.

①

①瑞士諾瓦士武術團來少林寺參禪

②日本不動禪代表團在少林武術館與少林弟子切磋武藝。

③學成歸國的德國拳師。

(1). A Swiss Shaolin kungfu delegation visits Shaolin Temple.

(2). Members of the Japanese Hudozen Wushu Delegation swop kungfu pointers with inhabitants of Shaolin Temple.

(3). German boxing practitioners have a picture taken after they have concluded their term of study at Shaolin Temple.

②

①

②

③

④

①來自異國的少林功夫愛好者在武術館學藝
②中國著名的高等學府——北京大學也成立了
　少林功夫研習班，並且吸引了外國留學生的
　興趣。
③成千上萬全國各地的中小學生來到嵩山脚下
　學習少林功夫
④少林功夫的揚名，使鄭州市的武術運動蓬勃
　而起，各類武術學校學員的武藝達到了相當
　水准。
⑤在少林寺所在的登封縣，各類武術學校衆多，
　在山坳之上經常可以看到這類演練場面。

(1). Shaolin kungfu lovers from foreign
lands learn martial arts at the wushu
guild.
(2). Foreign students are fascinated by
the Shaolin kungfu training course
opened at Beijing University.
(3). Tens of thousands of primary and
high school students come from all
over the country to learn wushu at
Shaolin Temple.
(4). The popularization of Shaolin kungfu
has promoted the rapid development
of wushu in Zhengzhou.
(5). Numerous wushu schools have been
established in Dengfeng County, in
which Shaolin Temple is located. It is
not uncommon to see people practice
wushu in the open field.

⑤

1986年建成的少林國際武術館，佔地4472平方米，爲少林功夫的推廣和普及提供了一個場所。圖爲武術館的學子在館前石階上演練少林單提腿功。

The completion of the 4,472-square-meter International Shaolin Wushu Guild in 1986 provides an ideal ground for the popularization of Shaolin kungfu. Picture shows beginners practicing holding up one leg at the side on the stone steps in front of the wushu guild.

③

④

⑤

①以武顯名的少林寺令嵩山旅遊熱方興未艾。
　1990年的少林武術節吸引了衆多賓客
②少林寺皈依弟子德虔大師應邀訪問新加坡，
　接受海外弟子的參拜。
③在少林寺，通讀佛經盡管不是一種必須的佛
　事活動，但却是武僧掌握佛理、培養德性的
　方式之一。
④閑暇之餘的消遣
⑤武僧們坐佛事

(1). The fame of Shaolin Temple set off a
tourist craze at Songshan Mountain.
The 1990 Shaolin Wushu Festival
attracted a great number of visitors.
(2). During his visit on invitation to
Singapore, master De Qian receives
overseas disciples who calls to pay
respects to him.
(3). Though the recitation of Buddhist
scripture is not a compulsory religious
activity, it is, however, one of the
ways for the fighting monks to learn
Buddhist doctrines and foster moral
integrity.
(4). In their leisure time.
(5). Fighting monks at a Buddhist service.

①

②

③

④

①以電影《少林寺》而聞名的功夫明星李連杰
②參加電影《少林寺》拍攝的全體真、假和尚
　合影於寺院門前。
③1982年上映的電影《少林寺》使海內外掀起
　了一股少林功夫熱。圖中為在少林寺塔林拍
　攝的一個鏡頭。
④電影《少林寺》中的一個鏡頭──少林僧大
　戰"禿鷹"。
⑤電影《少林俗家弟子》劇照。
⑥電影《少林小子》劇照
⑦電影《武當風雲》劇照

(1). Li Lianjie became a kungfu star when he played the leading part in the movie *Shaolin Temple*.
(2). Real and pretend monks particpating in the shooting of *Shaolin Temple* have a picture taken in front of the temple.
(3). After the movie was shown in 1982, Shaolin kungfu experienced a new wave of popularity both in and outside of China. Picture shows a scene from *Shaolin Temple* shot in the Forest of Pagodas beside the temple.
(4). Shaolin monks fight Bald Hawk, a scene from *Shaolin Temple*.
(5). A scene from the movie *Laymen Shaolin Kungfu Disciples*.
(6). A scene from *Little Monks of Shaolin Temple*.
(7). A scene from the movie *the Wudang Wushu School*.

⑤

⑥

⑦

# 鄭州風景名勝
# 示意圖

A sketch map showing
the historical and scenic spots in Zhengzhou

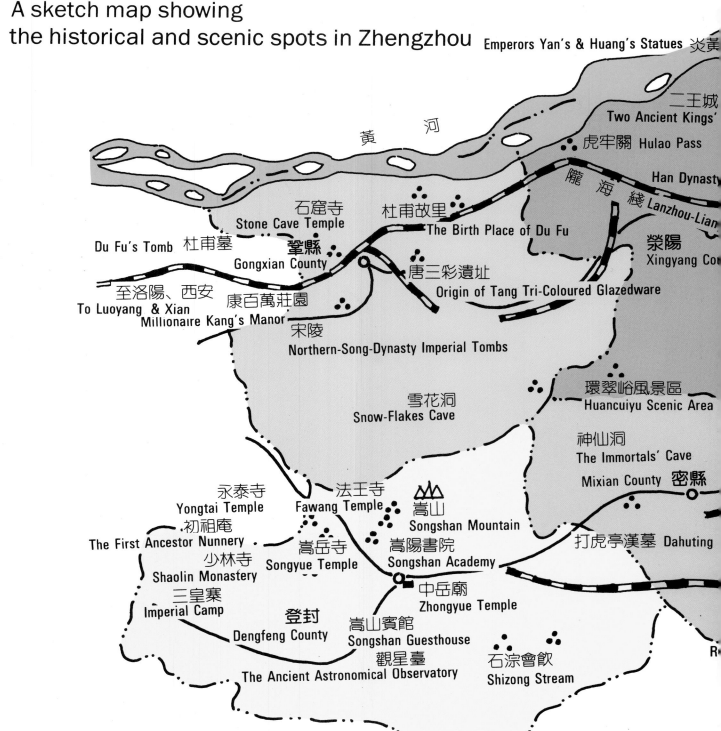

Emperors Yan's & Huang's Statues 炎黃

二王城
Two Ancient Kings'

黃　河

虎牢關 Hulao Pass

隴　海　綫 Lanzhou-Lian

Han Dynasty

石窟寺
Stone Cave Temple

杜甫故里
The Birth Place of Du Fu

滎陽
Xingyang Co

Du Fu's Tomb 杜甫墓

鞏縣
Gongxian County

唐三彩遺址
Origin of Tang Tri-Coloured Glazedware

至洛陽、西安
To Luoyang & Xian

康百萬莊園
Millionaire Kang's Manor

宋陵
Northern-Song-Dynasty Imperial Tombs

環翠峪風景區
Huancuiyu Scenic Area

雪花洞
Snow-Flakes Cave

神仙洞
The Immortals' Cave

Mixian County 密縣

永泰寺
Yongtai Temple

法王寺
Fawang Temple

嵩山
Songshan Mountain

初祖庵
The First Ancestor Nunnery

打虎亭漢墓 Dahuting

嵩岳寺
Songyue Temple

嵩陽書院
Songshan Academy

少林寺
Shaolin Monastery

三皇寨
Imperial Camp

中岳廟
Zhongyue Temple

登封
Dengfeng County

嵩山賓館
Songshan Guesthouse

觀星臺
The Ancient Astronomical Observatory

石淙會飲
Shizong Stream

R

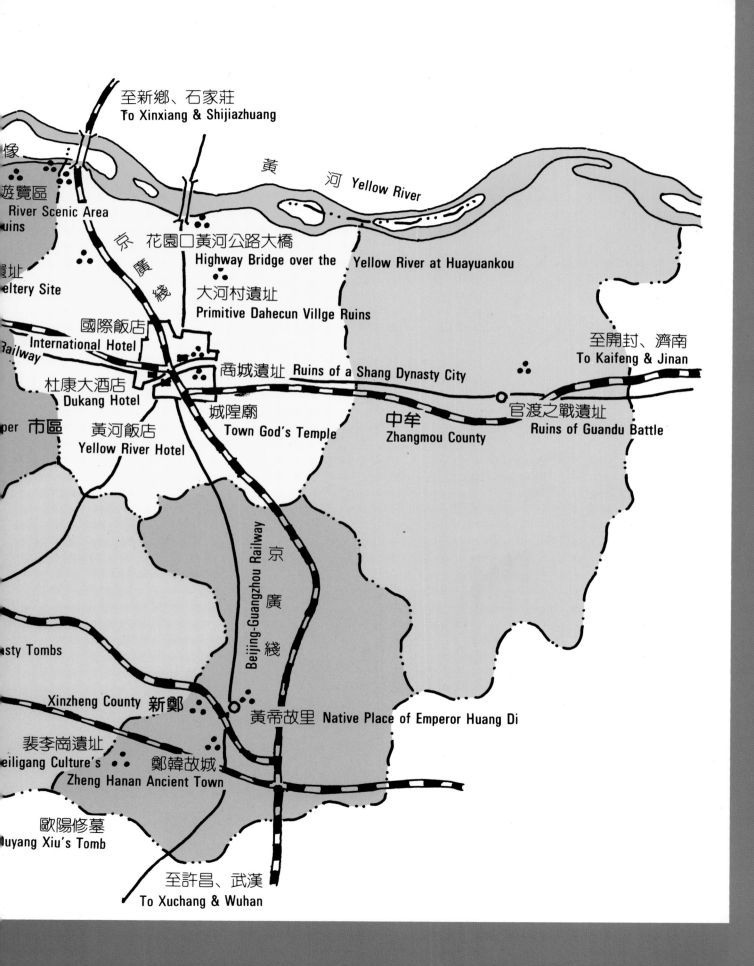

1926年少林寺主持、嵩山僧會司、少林寺保安團總恒林和尚所指揮的少林寺僧兵在大雄寶殿前舉行誓師大會。

In 1926, Heng Lin, then abbot of Shaolin Temple, secretary of the Songshan Monk Society and chief of the Shaolin Temple Security Corps, gathered the monk-soldiers to hold an oath-taking ritual in front of the temple's Mahavira Hall.

永祥和尚在少林寺被梵前（1927年）夏，抄的少林拳譜（共45卷）

*Shaolin Boxing Manual* (45 volumes in total), copied by monk Yong Xiang before he was burned to death at Shaolin Temple in the summer of 1927.

# 嵩山旅遊圖
## Tourist guide to Songshan Mountain

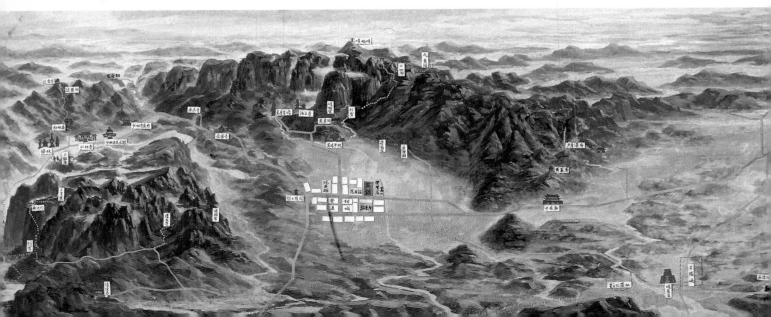

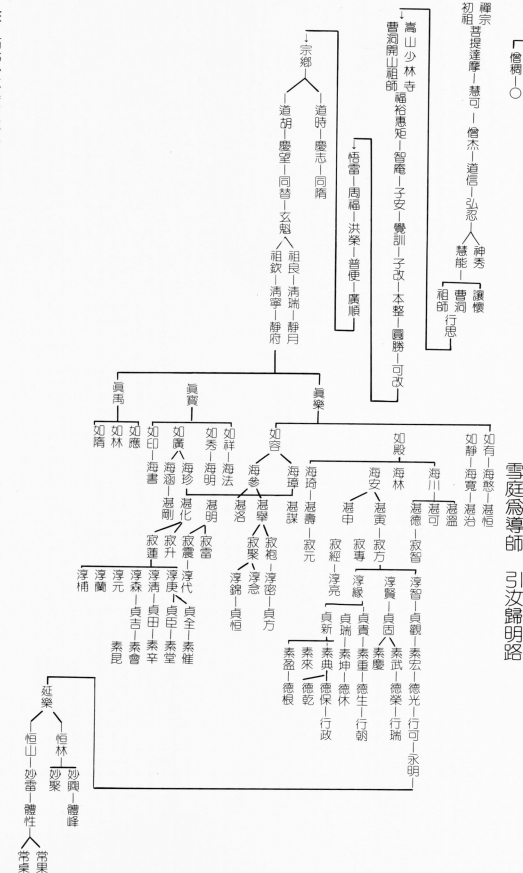

開山——禪宗——曹洞

山跋陀師
道房—○
慧光—○○
僧稠—○

禪宗
初祖菩提達摩—慧可—僧杰—道信—弘忍
　　　　　　　　　　　　　　　神秀
　　　　　　　　　　　　慧能—讓懷
　　　　　　　　　　　　　　　行思
　　　　　　　　　　　祖師—曹洞行思

嵩山少林寺福裕慧矩—智庵—子安—覺訓—子改—本整—圓勝—可改
曹洞開山祖師

## 嵩山少林寺曹洞正宗傳續七十字輩訣

福慧智子覺　子本圓可悟　周洪普廣宗　道慶同玄祖
清靜眞如海　湛寂淳貞素　德行永延恒　妙體常堅固
心朗照山深　性明鑒崇詐　忠正善禧祥　謹志原濟度
雪庭爲導師　引汝歸明路

註：右爲少林寺南院傳續宗譜
少林寺永化堂即南院宗師正道大和尚號雪居係江西豫章人，原在上藍寺出
家爲僧，屬臨濟派，於明代萬曆十五年率九賢徒子孫來嵩入曹洞正宗。

**图书在版编目(CIP)数据**

少林功夫：中英对照／邢雁等编辑，－北京：中国画报出版社，1996.5重印

ISBN 7－80024－196－3

I.少… II.邢… III.武术－中国－少林寺 IV.G852

中国版本图书馆CIP数据核字 (96) 第04675号

《少林功夫》

中国画报出版社　出版

精美彩色印刷有限公司　印刷

1996年5月第三次印刷

中国国际图书贸易总公司发行

中国北京车公庄西路35号

邮政信箱399号

邮政编码100044

**Shaolin Kungfu**

Published by China Pictorial Publishing House
Printed by the Jingmei Color Printing Co., Ltd.
Third printing: May 1996
Distributed by
China International Book Trading Corporation
35 Chegongzhuang Xilu Beijing 100044, China
P.O. Box 399, Beijing, China

ISBN7-80024-196-3

J · 197

07800

85CE－385P